TWENTIETH CENTURY VIEWS

The aim of this series is to present the best in contemporary critical opinion on major authors, providing a twentieth century perspective on their changing status in an era of profound revaluation.

Maynard Mack, *Series Editor*
Yale University

SHAKESPEARE THE HISTORIES

A COLLECTION OF CRITICAL ESSAYS

Edited by

Eugene M. Waith

A SPECTRUM BOOK

Prentice-Hall, Inc., *Englewood Cliffs, N. J.*

LIBRARY OF CONGRESS CATALOG CARD NO.: 65-11881

Printed in the United States of America—C

P 80770
C 80771

Table of Contents

Introduction

by Eugene M. Waith

    The first collected edition of Shakespeare's plays, the folio of 1623 brought out by his fellow actors, was entitled: *Mr. William Shakespeares Comedies, Histories, & Tragedies*; within the volume the "histories," from *King John* to *Henry VIII*, occupied the second of the three sections. The term was used during the playwright's lifetime for plays of very different sorts—for a dramatic biography such as *The Famous Historye of the life and death of Captaine Thomas Stukeley* or for a tragedy such as *The Tragicall History of the Life and Death of Doctor Faustus*—but above all for plays based on English chronicles. Shakespeare's plays based on Roman history were put with the tragedies, as were *King Lear* and *Macbeth*, based on what was supposed to be the early history of Britain and Scotland. For the folio editors Shakespeare's histories were plays dealing with the reigns of English sovereigns of the preceding four hundred years.

    The records leave us in no doubt that this kind of drama had been highly successful for the previous thirty years. In 1592 Thomas Nashe, referring presumably to Part I of Shakespeare's *Henry VI*, wrote a paean of appreciation: "How would it have joyed brave *Talbot* (the terror of the French) to thinke that after he had lyne two hundred yeares in his Tombe, hee should triumphe againe on the Stage. . . ." And in the same vein, concerning some pre-Shakespearian Henry V play: ". . . what a glorious thing it is to have *Henrie* the fifth represented on the Stage, leading the French King prisoner. . . ." [1] Both quotations show that unabashed patriotic fervor was one reason for the popularity of history plays. Furthermore, it accorded well with Renaissance poetics to suppose that English history on the stage would both warm English blood and inculcate virtue like any portrayal of the deeds of great men. A few

---

Some of the material of this introduction was presented in different form in a lecture delivered at Wayne State University, March 31st, 1964.

[1] From *Pierce Penilesse*, quoted by E. K. Chambers, *The Elizabethan Stage* (Oxford: The Clarendon Press, 1923), IV, 238-39.

years later Thomas Heywood made much of the didactic value of plays in his defense of the drama. He referred specifically to histories:

> . . . playes have made the ignorant more apprehensive, taught the unlearned the knowledge of many famous histories, instructed such as cannot reade in the discovery of all our *English* Chronicles: . . . Playes are writ with this ayme, and carryed with this methode, to teach the subjects obedience to their King, to shew the people the untimely ends of such as have moved tumults, commotions, and insurrections, to present them with the flourishing estate of such as live in obedience, exhorting them to allegeance, dehorting them from all trayterous and fellonious stratagems.[2]

Among the surviving plays on "modern" English history Shakespeare's ten bulk large. There is no doubt that historical themes absorbed his interest from the earliest years of his writing career to the latest, for he was either the sole author or the reviser of the Henry VI plays, performed in the early 1590's, and the author of part or all of *Henry VIII,* performed in 1613, when he had retired to Stratford. It may even be that Shakespeare was the originator of this popular form of drama, as F. P. Wilson[3] suggested several years ago. Leaving aside such special cases as Bale's *King Johan* (1530-36) and Legge's *Richardus Tertius* (1579), there appear to have been at most one or two plays comparable to Shakespeare's histories and performed before the Henry VI plays printed in the folio. That these are substantially Shakespeare's work has come to seem increasingly likely in recent years.[4] But even if he was refashioning the work of predecessors, as some critics have thought, it is clear from the angry gibe of his rival, Robert Greene, in 1592, that Shakespeare had set his mark upon these Henry VI plays and had a great success with them. In his famous passage of abuse Greene warns fellow playwrights against an "upstart Crow, beautified with our feathers" (by which he may have meant an actor-turned-playwright or a plagiarist) and one who thought himself "the only Shake-scene in a countrie." Adapting a line from *III Henry VI,* he spoke of "his *Tygers heart wrapt in a Players hide.*"[5] It is our first allusion to Shakespeare as a playwright.

The Elizabethan enthusiasm for history plays did not outlive Shakespeare by many years. While his unique position among Elizabethan

---

[2] *Apology for Actors* (1612), Scholars' Facsimiles & Reprints (New York, 1941), sigs. F3^r & ^v.

[3] *Marlowe and the Early Shakespeare* (Oxford: The Clarendon Press, 1953), p. 108.

[4] For a review of recent opinions on this subject, see the introductions by Andrew S. Cairncross to the Arden editions of *I Henry VI* (London: Methuen and Co. Ltd., 1962) and *II Henry VI* (1957).

[5] From *Greens Groats-worth of Wit,* quoted by E. K. Chambers, *op. cit.,* p. 241.

dramatists was being established by audiences and readers in the late seventeenth and eighteenth centuries, some of these plays were gradually slipping into oblivion. Those that held the stage did so for reasons having little to do with their special character as history plays: the role of Falstaff was a perennial attraction to actors as, until the end of the nineteenth century, the role of Richard III also was; for many years *Henry VIII* appealed to producers because of its pageantry. Critical interest during these years tended to focus on a character here or there—as in Maurice Morgann's notorious *Essay on the Dramatic Character of Sir John Falstaff* (1777) and in Coleridge's notes and lectures on *Richard II* —though there was occasional discerning comment on an entire play, notably Dr. Johnson's on *Henry IV*.

At the beginning of the twentieth century, George Pierce Baker observed in the course of a discussion of the history plays that only *Richard III* was often seen.[6] He saw them as interesting failures—a stage through which the maturing dramatist passed. A few years later Harley Granville-Barker, also looking for progress in dramaturgy, took a similar view. *Henry V* appeared to him to be an artistic dead end, since the portrayal of the personal feelings of the King was inadequate. In reading Baker and Granville-Barker one senses their conviction that the history plays are not "the real Shakespeare"—that his distinctive gifts were fully realized only in the comedies and tragedies. This opinion was held by many up to comparatively recent times, while among admirers of one or another of the histories there was a dismaying lack of agreement about which ones were to be admired.

One reason for disagreements and fluctuations of opinion was uncertainty about the nature of the history play. No classical genre showed what to expect of it, and something that was taken for granted by the Elizabethans became obscure for Augustans or Victorians. The obvious patriotic appeal provided no key to the structure or characterization. For some twentieth century critics it was one reason more for adopting a somewhat patronizing attitude toward the plays. They were, perhaps, the kind of thing that people in a simpler, cruder age enjoyed.

There is a striking contrast between such attitudes as these, current in the earlier years of this century, and the present admiration for the history plays. They are being performed with increasing frequency, and they have been written about intensively for three decades. Their stock has probably never been so high since Shakespeare's death. The explanation for this revolution in taste lies in the renewed understanding of

---

[6] *The Development of Shakespeare as a Dramatist* (New York: The Macmillan Company, 1907), p. 148.

theme and structure provided by several twentieth century scholars. Selections from their work appear in this volume. Its significance can best be appreciated by examining the approaches they used to bring about so radical a revaluation.[7]

The chief requisite for an understanding of Shakespeare's histories proved to be, logically enough, a full awareness of Elizabethan attitudes toward history. Their central belief that history teaches lessons for the present is familiar today, but the suggestion of familiarity is deceptive, for their total concept of history seems more strange the further its ramifications are pursued. One notices the extraordinarily lofty position reserved for it. Louis Wright states that "The Elizabethan citizen shared the belief of his learned and courtly contemporaries that the reading of history was an exercise second only to a study of Holy Writ in its power to induce good morality and shape the individual into a worthy member of society." [8] The comparison with the Bible is anything but fortuitous. As Lily B. Campbell and E. M. W. Tillyard pointed out, history and theology were intimately associated in the Elizabethan mind. Political convictions also gave distinctive shape to the concept of history. Thus, to provide the intellectual background for an interpretation of the plays it was necessary to study sixteenth century historiography in its relations to Reformation theology and political theory.

A beginning had already been made in the nineteenth century. In spite of the prevailing opinions, some scholars had begun to suspect that the history plays were not merely patriotic pageants ennobled by a few penetrating studies of character. Here and there the suggestion was made that the plays contained coherent political thinking, though to some admirers of the Bard this was to accuse him of triviality. In an influential book written early in this century, Tucker Brooke wrote: "The Henry IV and Henry V plays form a closely connected series presenting a well-matured theory of royal responsibility and governmental ethics by means of their picture of the character evolution of a great national leader." [9] The emphasis still fell heavily upon character but a dominant political theme was recognized. Two historians went into greater detail. Sir J. A. R. Marriott wrote that "National unity was to Shakespeare the one supreme

---

[7] For a survey of twentieth century scholarship on the history plays see Harold Jenkins, "Shakespeare's History Plays: 1900-1951," *Shakespeare Survey*, VI (1953), 1-15. Rather than attempt anything so comprehensive, I have concentrated in the remarks that follow on the chief sorts of contribution that have enlarged our understanding.

[8] *Middle-Class Culture in Elizabethan England* (Ithaca, New York: Cornell University Press, 1958), p. 297. (First published 1935.)

[9] *The Tudor Drama* (Boston, New York, Chicago: Houghton Mifflin Company, 1911), p. 332.

condition of national greatness," and that "The great speech of Ulysses in *Troilus and Cressida* may indeed be taken as a summary embodiment of his political creed." He saw that Shakespeare had used not only Holinshed's *Chronicles,* as had long been known, but also Hall's *The Union of the Two Noble and Illustrious Families of York and Lancaster,* which dealt with the exact period covered in the tetralogies, *Richard II* to *Henry V* and *Henry VI* to *Richard III.*[10] C. L. Kingsford was also interested in the connection with Hall, and saw that his view of the War of the Roses was the very one that underlay Shakespeare's cycle, though he drew back from the suggestion that "Shakespeare wrote with this idea definitely before him." [11] In 1929 H. B. Charlton lectured to The English Association about "Shakespeare, Politics, and Politicians," asserting the predominance of political themes in the history plays. Though he excluded *Richard III* and *Richard II* from this category as plays too much concerned with individuals, he anticipated later critics with his comment (p. 11), "The real hero of the English history-play is England."

A more thorough investigation of these matters was undertaken in the 1930's and 1940's, the period of the most influential research on the histories. By then it was being further stimulated by two special sorts of study, which cannot be represented in this volume. New and controversial theories about the transmission of dramatic texts were persuading many scholars of Shakespeare's responsibility for all of the Henry VI plays. The existence of some underlying theme in the *Henry VI–Richard III* tetralogy thus became more credible, and a way was opened for the consideration of a grand scheme including the other tetralogy, *Richard II–Henry V,* written later but dealing with the earlier period of history. Closely related to these textual studies were the new editions of Shakespeare, among which J. Dover Wilson's deserves special mention. His introductions to the history volumes, like his *Fortunes of Falstaff,* from which selections are reprinted here, were both learned and provocative.

Some of the most important work on the background of the histories was done by Lily B. Campbell and E. M. W. Tillyard. First in articles and later in a book, Miss Campbell showed how prevailing concepts of history influenced Tudor historians. Since the historical process was a working out of the divine will, they sought to reveal that pattern in their accounts of English wars, domestic or foreign, and to assign blame for

---

[10] *English History in Shakespeare* (London: Chapman & Hall, 1918), pp. 5, 12, 28.

[11] "Fifteenth Century History in Shakespeare's Plays," *Prejudice & Promise in XVth Century England* (Oxford: The Clarendon Press, 1925), p. 3. This lecture is a revision of an undated pamphlet in the National Home-Reading Union Series, probably published in 1915.

such catastrophic events as the War of the Roses. Hall saw the deposition
of Richard II as the origin of the disturbances which ended only when
the sin of Henry IV was expiated by Richard III. In this case the role
of the first Tudor king, Henry VII, in ending the war and re-establishing
order became the basis of the so-called "Tudor myth," which presented
the reigning dynasty as heaven-appointed saviors of their country. Here
the connection between religious and political belief in such a view of
history is particularly clear. As Miss Campbell showed, a most important
corollary was that the moral pattern of history could and should provide
answers to the immediate problems of governmental policy. Contemporary situations could be seen in the mirror of history, where the actions
of good and bad rulers in the past served as timely lessons for their
successors. If history was written on these principles, it was reasonable to
suppose that history plays had a keen topical interest for their audiences,
and Miss Campbell suggested that each play was contrived to refer to
contemporary events—to plots and uprisings familiar to everyone.[12] Both
she and Tillyard showed how the fear of Catholic plots against the Protestant sovereigns led to the homilies on obedience read in churches, for
as Christopher Morris[13] and others have pointed out, Protestantism was
at this time a main bulwark of the power and authority of the monarch.
Such a policy as this was clearly relevant to the problem of usurpation
posed in Shakespeare's plays.

Tillyard was especially interested in the connection between the concept of political order and the hierarchical view of cosmic order commonly accepted in Shakespeare's day. In *The Elizabethan World Picture*,
published before his study of the history plays, he described the elaborate
correspondences in this standard view, which related the actions of men
to the motions of the stars.[14] In the history plays no less than in the
tragedies, universal meanings attached to the decisions of great men. In
his later book Tillyard, like Marriott before him, used the speech of
Ulysses in *Troilus and Cressida* as a key to the theme of order in the
history plays. He believed that the two tetralogies, covering the period
from Richard II to Richard III, made "a single unit," though not written
in chronological sequence, and that they dramatized the view of this

---

[12] *Shakespeare's "Histories": Mirrors of Elizabethan Policy* (San Marino, California:
Huntington Library, 1947), p. 125.

[13] *Political Thought in England* (London, New York, Toronto: Geoffrey Cumberlege,
Oxford University Press, 1953), Chaps. 1-4; see also Alfred Hart, *Shakespeare and the
Homilies* (Melbourne: Melbourne University Press, 1934).

[14] (London: Chatto & Windus, 1943), esp. pp. 81-93; see also Theodore Spencer,
Shakespeare and the Nature of Man (New York: The Macmillan Company, 1942) and
Hardin Craig, *The Enchanted Glass* (New York: Oxford University Press, 1936).

period derived from Hall.[15] The suggestion that these eight plays had a structure of such complexity and scope encouraged a reconsideration of the artistic merits of all the histories. It was no longer possible to condescend to them as historical vignettes loosely strung together.

Another important part of the background of the histories was their literary and dramatic ancestry. Miss Campbell showed how heavily indebted they were to *A Mirror for Magistrates,* the popular sixteenth century work in which the "falls of famous men" were made to instruct living rulers.[16] Several scholars saw that the form of the histories could be traced back to medieval mystery plays, which presented Old and New Testament history, and to morality plays, in which the moral encounters of mankind were represented allegorically. A number of sixteenth century plays applied this allegorical technique to history and thus built up a dramatic tradition for the presentation of the lessons of history. Closely related were the welcoming pageants set up in city streets, such as the emblematic show of "The uniting of the two houses of Lancastre and Yorke" presented to Queen Elizabeth during her coronation procession. Here the lesson was very similar to that of the conclusion of Shakespeare's *Richard III.* The garden scene in *Richard II* demonstrates the continuing vitality of the allegorical tradition, and an important aspect of Falstaff stands out more sharply when we see him as Dover Wilson did (see "Falstaff and the Prince," in this volume) as an embodiment of Riot and Feasting. The morality plays provided examples of a kind of drama where theme rather than story determined the organization. Their "parentage" of the history plays suggested that the themes discussed by Miss Campbell and Tillyard might be far more important in shaping those plays than the sequence of events that constitute their outward structure. In an illuminating discussion of this line of development, A. P. Rossiter proposed the term "moral history" as "a useful name for history-plays where the shadow-show of a greater drama of state plays continually behind the human characters, sometimes (as in Shakespeare) upon something as large as the cyclorama of the stars." [17]

By about the middle of this century, then, the basis for a new approach to Shakespeare's histories had been firmly established. The kinds of background study just described are represented in the first three selections in this anthology: Miss Campbell's discussion of historiography, Tillyard's of the Elizabethan world order, and the concise account by M. M. Reese

---

[15] *Shakespeare's History Plays* (New York: The Macmillan Company, 1946), pp. 147 ff.

[16] See her edition of the *Mirror for Magistrates* (Cambridge: The University Press, 1938) and *Shakespeare's "Histories,"* pp. 106-16.

[17] *Woodstock, A Moral History* (London: Chatto & Windus, 1946), p. 9.

of literary and dramatic precedents. The interpretations of individual plays that follow reflect an awareness of Tudor attitudes toward history, of the legacy of the morality plays and *A Mirror for Magistrates,* and of the contemporary political situation. However, the authors of some of these essays disagree with certain interpretations of Shakespeare advanced by Miss Campbell or Tillyard or Dover Wilson. Derek Traversi, for example, says: "The increased attention now given to the background of the plays in terms of contemporary political thought, though in many ways illuminating, has not been without dangers of its own." Some of these dangers are specified by others who share Traversi's misgivings. Irving Ribner writes: "What Tillyard says of Shakespeare is largely true, but by limiting the goals of the serious play within the narrow framework of Hall's particular view, he compresses the wide range of Elizabethan historical drama into entirely too narrow a compass. There were other schools of historiography in Elizabethan England." [18] L. C. Knights makes a similar objection, that Shakespeare's politics were not simply the Elizabethan world picture, and M. M. Reese, emphasizing the "many-sidedness of his vision," says, "Shakespeare was a poet, not a writer of political tracts." [19] C. L. Barber in his widely reprinted study of *Henry IV,* sees that Falstaff was not wholly condemned in the role of the King of Misrule or Riot or Feasting, but also represented positive qualities which had been traditionally celebrated.[20]

Criticism along these lines has provided useful correctives. Full justice cannot be done to the *Richard II–Henry V* tetralogy without introducing other concepts than retribution for Henry IV's sin of usurpation, nor do the political lessons implied in the parallels to contemporary events account adequately for the themes of these plays. The debate about Shakespeare's political thinking continues, but the view of Shakespeare as orthodox though not doctrinaire appears to be gaining wider acceptance. The plays reveal a passionate concern with the problems of rulership and order in the common weal. They may not teach as specific lessons as once was claimed.

Indeed the connections that various critics now see between the histories and the plays written after them lead in the opposite direction

---

[18] *The English History Play in the Age of Shakespeare* (Princeton, New Jersey: Princeton University Press, 1957), p. 12.

[19] L. C. Knights, "Shakespeare's Politics," *Proceedings of the British Academy* (1957), pp. 115-32; M. M. Reese, *The Cease of Majesty* (London: Edward Arnold (Publishers) Ltd., 1961), p. viii.

[20] "Rule and Misrule in *Henry IV,*" *Shakespeare's Festive Comedy* (Princeton, New Jersey: Princeton University Press, 1959), pp. 192-221.

from clear-cut answers. Traversi, in a study of the Roman plays, has recently suggested that the second tetralogy prepares in certain ways for *Antony and Cleopatra,* and Ernest Schanzer has made a similar observation.[21] The tragedies of Shakespeare's later years, the period that Willard Farnham calls his "tragic frontier," are characterized by a puzzling ambivalence. "Taints and honors" wage equal, and what seem to be glaring faults are also virtues. The history plays seem to lead up to this kind of presentation of character. Richard II is a dangerously weak king, though a terrible price is to be paid for deposing him; Henry is a wicked usurper but a very capable monarch. All these contradictory truths are to be accepted. As Clifford Leech has said, "We travel two roads, or more, at once." [22]

Both the virtues and the limitations of background studies are well illustrated by what they have contributed to the understanding of the history plays. They have provided invaluable material, without which the current revaluation would hardly have taken place, but if the background is made to determine the entire meaning, we are in danger of losing the very thing that distinguishes one author from another—his *treatment* of the traditional themes.

An appreciation of the complexity within the unified structure of Shakespeare's histories has been greatly aided by studies of their imagery. It is frequently pointed out that such studies run the danger of treating plays as poems, but though the warning is salutary, it should not suggest that the method is invalid. Since there is no true dichotomy between plays and poems, the fact that Shakespeare's plays are eminently actable, even eminently theatrical, does not prevent them from being poems in the sense of intricately organized verbal artifacts. The best studies of imagery in the history plays have shown how intimately verbal patterns are bound with theatrical effect. The essay by R. J. Dorius included in this volume is an excellent example. He discusses the significance of the images of fatness and disease in *Richard II* and *Henry IV* and reminds us that such images assault our eyes directly in the person of "plump Jack Falstaff." Others have commented on the imagery of rising and falling in *Richard II,*[23] reflecting the basic structure of the play and dramatized in the Flint Castle scene, where the King comes "down like glistering

[21] Derek Traversi, *Shakespeare: The Roman Plays* (Stanford, California: Stanford University Press, 1963), pp. 9-18; Ernest Schanzer, *The Problem Plays of Shakespeare* (New York: Schocken Books, 1963), pp. 162-67.

[22] "The Unity of 2 *Henry IV*," *Shakespeare Survey,* VI (1953), 23.

[23] See Paul Jorgenson, "Vertical Patterns in *Richard II,*" *Shakespeare Association Bulletin,* XXIII (1948), 119-34.

Phaeton." Verbal and theatrical imagery collaborate with other elements
of Shakespeare's dramaturgy to force us to grasp the historical situations
in their wholeness.

Another profitable kind of verbal analysis has become more frequent
recently—the discussion of rhetorical patterns. The highly formal style
of certain scenes in early history plays, for example, can be shown to
serve several purposes. In his essay on *Richard III* in this anthology, A. P.
Rossiter comments that the "notional pattern of historic events rigidly
determined by a mechanical necessity is partly paralleled by, partly modified by, the formal patterns of the episodes (or scenes) and the language."
Where this style is most conspicuous—in the first tetralogy, in Henry IV's
speech on sleep, in the farewells of Buckingham and Wolsey in *Henry
VIII*—it both intensifies and distances the emotions presented. The effect
is singularly appropriate to the mixed response which these plays seem to
demand.

Now that the histories have again taken their place with the comedies
and tragedies as a thoroughly respectable and even admired third division of Shakespeare's plays, one would expect to find that scholars had
agreed upon some definition of the genre. In fact this is not the case. In
spite of all the light that has been thrown on the nature of these plays,
it has not ended discussion of what distinguishes a history from any other
kind of play. Coleridge made a useful distinction among the Shakespearian plays containing historical material. It did not depend "on the quantity of historical events compared with the fictions, for there is as much
history in *Macbeth* as in *Richard,* but in the relation of the history to
the plot. In the purely historical plays, the history *informs* the plot; in
the mixt [a category that Coleridge devised for *Henry IV*] it *directs* it;
in the rest, as *Macbeth, Hamlet, Cymbeline, Lear,* it subserves it." The
relative importance of historical themes is well suggested here, though
despite the prominence of comic scenes in *Henry IV,* there is no reason
to deny that history "informs" its plot. The important distinction is
between the "purely historical" and the plays in Coleridge's last category,
where history "subserves" the plot and other interests predominate. Miss
Campbell gives the most useful account of the difference between these
interests: ". . . it is to this distinction between private and public morals
that we must look for the distinction between tragedy and history. Tragedy is concerned with the doings of men which in philosophy are discussed under *ethics;* history with the doings of men which in philosophy
are discussed under *politics.*" [24] The material and even many of the
themes of *King Lear* and *Macbeth* are identical with those of history

---

[24] *Shakespeare's "Histories,"* p. 17.

plays, but the dominant concern is with private morals—with what an individual chooses to do. On the other hand, though the personal tragedy of Richard II is emphasized and made very touching, especially in the last act, we are never allowed to forget the larger issues of which it is a part. Richard is presented as one term of an extended comparison between weak legitimacy and strong usurpation.

The way in which the play focuses attention on one or the other of these concerns can be illustrated by a further comparison. The endings of *Richard III* and *Macbeth* are strikingly similar. Each of the heroes makes a dogged final stand: "I have set my life upon a cast/And I will stand the hazard of the die," says Richard (V, 4, 9-10);[25] and Macbeth: "They have tied me to a stake. I cannot fly,/But bear-like I must fight the course" (V, 7, 1-2). Each is then defeated in battle by the champion of order, who comes to purge the kingdom. Richmond points to the body of "this bloody wretch" (V, 5, 5), and Malcolm to the head of "this dead butcher" (V, 8, 69). Yet the meanings of these two deaths are far from identical. Macbeth's final battle is preceded by the scene in which he hears the "cry of women" and receives the news that Lady Macbeth has died. He comments on his hardened sensibilities—the result of "supping full with horrors"—and then, in one of the most famous speeches in dramatic literature, shows how the hardening process has been accompanied by disillusionment. He has deliberately suppressed moral awareness, but his perception is still keen enough to give him a nightmare vision of emptiness and meaninglessness—a "tale told by an idiot." The spectator cannot view the death of such a hero in a purely historical perspective. The horror of Macbeth's reduction to this state of mind colors the entire finale.

To Macbeth's "Tomorrow, and tomorrow" speech corresponds Richard's soliloquy as he wakes from the dream in which the ghosts of his victims appeared to him. It is a long debate with himself, formally patterned like a catechism:

> What do I fear? Myself? There's none else by.
> Richard loves Richard: that is, I am I.
> Is there a murtherer here? No. Yes, I am.
> Then fly. What from myself?
>
> [V, 3, 183-86]

The highly rhetorical style sacrifices a sense of inwardness to the clarity of the point it is making: that the King's self-love is fighting off fear and

---

[25] Reference is to *The Complete Works of Shakespeare,* ed. G. L. Kittredge (Boston: Ginn and Company, 1936).

guilt. His control of his feelings is outwardly more shaken than Macbeth's, and at one point he even says he will despair, but we are not given the sense that the abyss has opened for him as it has for Macbeth. Between Richard's soliloquy and the battle come his speeches to his army, which have no equivalent in *Macbeth*. It is obvious there that self-love has won the fight with fear and guilt and that the King is once more a clever and eloquent spokesman for immorality. To his nobles he says:

> Let not our babbling dreams affright our souls;
> For conscience is a word that cowards use . . .
> March on, join bravely, let us to't pell-mell,
> If not to heaven, then hand in hand to hell.

> [V, 3, 309-10, 313-14]

The soldiers get less moral philosophy and more appeal to their vanity, their fears, and their prejudices. These are good, shouting exhortations. The mode of public address inclines us to view Richard mainly as a public figure, and even his soliloquy does more to type him than to give us an intimate view. Hence, when his end comes, it has the significance of the downfall of the tyrant. Despite the fact that Richard completely dominates the play, and that he has a sinister fascination, we are enabled to accept Richmond's view of him entirely and rejoice that he has been put out of the way. The significance of Richard III's life and death lies in the effect they have upon England. The meaning of the play points not inward, as in *Macbeth*, but outward to a world of political concerns.

A major revaluation of an artistic work ordinarily follows a renewed understanding of the mode in which the work was created. The impulse leading to such a rediscovery is likely to be rooted in the particular needs and interests of the discoverers, so that while they may reveal lasting truths about the work in question, they also find there something of themselves. The revaluation of metaphysical poetry in the first quarter of our century clearly reflected certain aspects of our own sensibility, and no doubt the same may be said of the revaluation of Shakespeare's histories. Their dramatic posing of questons to which no simple answer exists, their faithfulness to the complexity of the issues, and their concern with the responsibility of the ruler to his country recommend themselves to an age beset by enormous political problems—an age more than normally aware of bewildering multiplicity and less than normally certain that there are answers to every question.

English History in
the Sixteenth Century

by Lily B. Campbell

C. L. Kingsford terminated his study of *English Historical Literature in the Fifteenth Century* at 1485, appending a chapter on the sixteenth-century histories. No more adequate work has appeared, and the several general histories of historiography which have been published in recent years give very spare accounts of the Tudor histories.[1] Professor Harry Elmer Barnes, for instance, in one of the latest of these works gives just a little over one page to the subject of "humanist historiography in England," and he mentions—and barely mentions—only Polydore Vergil, Sir Thomas More, Sir Walter Raleigh, William Camden, and Francis Bacon. Fueter in his more comprehensive survey of modern historiography devotes twelve pages to the English Renaissance and is the only one of these writers to link English historical writing to various movements on the Continent. But to the histories which are perhaps most important to the study of the literature of the period and certainly most important to the study of Shakespeare he gives only one short paragraph . . . .

There are undoubtedly two reasons for this neglect of the popular and influential English chronicles. In the first place, the historian of history

"English History in the Sixteenth Century." From *Shakespeare's "Histories": Mirrors of Elizabethan Policy* (San Marino, California: Huntington Library, 1947), by Lily B. Campbell, pp. 55-80. Copyright 1947 by The Henry E. Huntington Library and Art Gallery. Reprinted by permission of the author and The Henry E. Huntington Library and Art Gallery. Three quotations from Fueter have been omitted as well as the treatment of several historians of the late sixteenth century.

[1] The latest is J. W. Thompson, *A History of Historical Writing* (New York, 1942). The best for this period and the only one much concerned with the philosophy of history is that of E. Fueter (*Histoire de l'historiographie*), referred to many times in these pages. Conyers Read, *Bibliography of British History: Tudor Period, 1485-1603* (Oxford, 1933) is here as always in Tudor studies a trustworthy guide. Bishop W. Nicolson in his *English, Scotch and Irish Historical Libraries* (London, 1776) made an interesting beginning, which is yet useful. See also L. B. Wright, *Middle-Class Culture in Elizabethan England* (Chapel Hill, 1935), Chap. ix.

is dependent on a mass of detailed scholarship which is not yet available concerning these English works. In the second place, he is usually intent upon detecting the emergence of new ideas and especially the emergence of those new ideas which have prevailed and which are now accepted. Like most of the literary critics who are today giving allegiance to "the history of ideas," he is trying to trace the source from which today's ideas have come. That is to say, he is primarily interested not in discovering what succeeding generations thought about history or how they wrote history, but in tracing the origins of what we today hold worthy or even of what he himself today holds worthy.[2] The literary historian, on the other hand, approaches the study of history, as he does that of any other form of writing, from the past rather than from the present. He tries to see what were its purposes and its methods in succeeding generations. It is solely from this point of view, then, that I propose to examine the histories of England published and written during the Tudor period. It is needless to say, I hope, that a review of these works in a single chapter presents merely a sampling of the whole. But there is so much that is common to all as far as method and purpose are concerned that it does not seem necessary to eat the whole firkin in order to judge the butter.

The Tudor sovereigns were responsible, directly and indirectly, for much of the determination to write anew the history of England during their reigns. However, the printing press, still new when Henry VII was crowned, had already made and continued to make certain histories of an older period available. The *Polychronicon* of Higden in Trevisa's translation, first published in 1482, contains a "Proheyme" particularly interesting as showing what may be called the continuity of historical theory, for it calls history a perpetual conservator of the past, the giver of immortality to both good and evil, fame and infamy. It praises history as the mother of philosophy and the nurse of good learning, and argues that though poets have by their fables undertaken to inflame the "courages" of men, though laws and institutions have tried to punish men into goodness, it is history that has proved the most effective teacher. And significantly, it parallels two undertakings, this history of a secular kind, and the *Golden Legend* with its accounts of the lives, miracles, passions, and deaths of divers holy saints.

But our concern here is with the histories published or written under the Tudors, and since, as Kingsford says, the chronicle of Fabyan is to

---

[2] Preserved Smith, for instance, in his *Age of the Reformation* (1920) said: "It is hard to see any value, save occasionally as sources, in the popular English chronicles of Edward Hall, Raphael Holinshed, and John Stow. Full of court gossip and of pageantry, strongly royalist, conservative and patriotic, they reflect the interests of the middle-class cockney as faithfully as does a certain type of newspaper and magazine today."

be regarded as the last of the fifteenth-century histories rather than the earliest of the sixteenth century, I propose to begin with the *Chronicle* of John Hardyng, first published in 1543 with a continuation in prose by Richard Grafton.[3] The preface recites many of the commonplaces concerning history, but I call attention to one stanza particularly which records the divine endorsement of history:

> Wherfore Goddes woorde and holy scripture
> Which abandoneth all maner vanitee
> Yet of Chronicles admitteth the lecture
> As a thing of great fruite and utilitee
> And as a lanterne, to the posteritee
> For example, what they ought to knowe
> What waies to refuse, and what to folowe.

The "Proheme" to "My lorde of Yorke" points out the general lessons of history taught therein. The comment on Henry IV, for instance, calls attention to one of the divine laws to be expounded at length by Raleigh much later:

> For when Henry the fourth first was crouned
> Many a wyseman, sayd then full commenly
> The third heyre shuld not joyse but be uncrouned
> And deposed of all regalitee
> To this reason they dyd there wittes applye,
> Of evill gotten good, the third should not enjoyse
> Of longe agone, it hath bene a commen voyce.

But new works were to be written, and the first Tudor king, Henry VII, set himself to the task by engaging the services of two foreigners, Bernard André and Polydore Vergil. Dr. William Nelson in his recent study of the scholars whom Henry VII brought to his court stresses the king's recognition of history as "the princely subject *par excellence*" and offers an illustration:

Claude De Seyssel, the French ambassador, could find no more appropriate gift for Henry VII than a French translation of Xenophon, royally inscribed on vellum. In the dedication De Seyssel says that King Henry has a splendid

---

[3] For an account of the two variant editions by Grafton in the same year and the history of Hardyng's manuscript versions see C. L. Kingsford, "The First Version of Hardyng's Chronicle," in the *English Historical Review*, XXVII (1912), 462-82.

library and enjoys both hearing and reading histories and other matters fit
for a wise and noble prince. He is an experienced ruler, both in peace and in
war, and will therefore recognize the value of the practical advice and warn-
ings to be found in Xenophon's *Anabasis,* a work which, in the opinion of
King Louis XII of France, should be divulged only to princes and to great
personages.[4]

This work had been given to Louis XII, who, Dr. Nelson says, wished to
be the sole possessor of such a rare treasure, but Henry's kindness to De
Seyssel was so great that a second copy was made. I have already spoken
of De Seyssel in connection with the translation of Thucydides by
Nicolls,[5] but it must be emphasized here that King Henry VII, anxious
as he was to bring England abreast of the new learning on the continent,
could scarcely have failed to be impressed by the interests of the French
ambassador, who was to his own king a sort of translator-general of the
ancient histories.

Bernard André had been teaching at Oxford before he was appointed
tutor to the king's eldest child, Prince Arthur, and the thorough ground-
ing in history which the young prince received is evidenced in André's
statement that by the time he was sixteen Arthur "had either committed
to memory or read with his own eyes and leafed with his own fingers"
Thucydides, Livy, Caesar, Suetonius, Tacitus, Pliny, Valerius Maximus,
Sallust, and Eusebius.[6] After four years as tutor André was appointed
to write the life of Henry VII and was generously rewarded, apparently
on a yearly basis. He kept records of current events in the form of annals.

But it was Polydore Vergil's appointment to write a history of England
that was for English historiography the most important event of the reign
of Henry VII.[7] Vergil came to the English court about 1501 as a papal
envoy, but for fifty years he remained in England, where he gained pre-
ferment and ultimately was naturalized. When he appointed Vergil to
write a history of England, Henry VII was, as the Tudors continued to be,
much concerned with finding King Arthur on the family tree. However,
Vergil's work was not published until 1534, when Henry VIII had suc-

---

[4] "The Scholars of Henry VII" in *John Skelton: Laureate* (New York, 1939), p. 23.
[5] See [L. B. Campbell, *Shakespeare's "Histories"*], pp. 44-45.
[6] Nelson, *op. cit.,* p. 15.
[7] The basis for most modern accounts of Vergil is the preface of Sir Henry Ellis in
his edition of *Three Books of Polydore Vergil's English History* (London, 1844) published for the Camden Society (Vol. XXIX). Other accounts will be found in Kingsford,
Fueter, Thompson, etc. Of special interest is the article by E. A. Whitney and P. P.
Cram, "The Will of Polydore Vergil," in the *Royal Historical Society Transactions,*
Fourth Series, XI, 117-36, where a list of editions with some account of Vergil's influence
on later English writers is to be found.

ceeded his father, and instead of bolstering the Tudor claims, it attacked the historicity of Arthur. The result was a battle of books which has been the subject of much recent scholarship,[8] and a defamation of Vergil's character which has not yet received adequate unprejudiced appraisal. But these matters are not of importance here. What is important is that Vergil was the first of the humanist historians to write the history of England. As Kingsford pointed out, he is regarded as the first to break publicly in England with the long tradition of a purely annalistic form of history. On the positive side, Sir Henry Ellis said of his work:

> It was the first of our histories in which the writer ventured to compare the facts and weigh the statements of his predecessors; and it was the first in which summaries of personal character are introduced in the terse and energetic form adopted in the Roman classics.[9]

But it must be remembered that Vergil wrote in Latin, and that the nine editions of his work to 1651 were all published on the Continent. It made a knowledge of English history accessible to readers outside England, but it did not provide the mass of English people directly with a history of their own land.

Indirectly, by furnishing Halle and later English writers with much of their material, Vergil contributed greatly to the writing of English history for popular consumption. He wrote history as a connected, unified narrative, relating cause and effect, interpreting events, generalizing their significance so that they might serve as useful lessons ever capable of new application, and in so doing he set the pattern for the popular chronicles. I quote from the sixteenth-century translation of his work (which was not published until the nineteenth century), by way of illustrating these characteristics. In chronicling the terrible dream of Richard III on the night before the battle of Bosworth Field, for instance, he comments:

> But (I beleve) yt was no dreame, but a conscyence guiltie of haynous offences, a conscyence (I say) so muche the more grevous as thoffences wer more great, which, thowght at none other time, yeat in the last day of owr lyfe ys woont to represent to us the memory of our sinnes commyttyd, and withall to shew unto us the paynes immynent for the same, that, being uppon good cause penytent at that instant for our evell led lyfe, we may be compellyd to go hence in heavynes of hart.[10]

[8] The pioneer study was made by Edwin Greenlaw in a paper on "The Battle of the Books," published in *Studies in Spenser's Historical Allegory* (Baltimore, 1932). See also C. B. Millican, *Spenser and the Table Round* (Cambridge, Mass., 1932).

[9] *Op. cit.*, p. xxviii.

[10] *Ibid.*, p. 222.

Again, telling how Edward IV won protection in York by promising
under oath to treat the citizens well and to be an obedient and faithful
servant of King Henry VI thenceforth, even as he was plotting to deprive
that king of his throne, Vergil moralizes:

> Thus oftentimes as well men of highe as of low cawling blynded with covet-
> ousnes, and forgetting al religyon and honesty, ar woont to make promyse
> in swearing by thimmortal God, which promyse neverthelesse they ar already
> determynyd to breake before they make yt. Of this matter yt shall not yrk me
> to make mentyon in the lyfe of king Richerd the third . . . , wher perchaunce
> yt may be well conceavyed that thissew of king Edward did partycypate also
> the fault of this perjury.[11]

And when he describes the murder of the little princes by Richard III,
he repeats the moral and enlarges upon it:

> What man ys ther in this world, who, yf he have regard unto suche noble
> children thus shamefully murderid, wyll not tremble and quake, seing that
> suche matters often happen for thoffences of our ancestors, whose faults doo
> redownd to the posterytie? That fortunyd peradventure to these two innocent
> impes because Edward ther fathyr commytted thoffence of perjury, . . . and
> for that afterwardes, by reason of his brother the duke of Clarence death, he
> had chargyd himself and his posterytie before God with dew desert of grevous
> punysshement.[12]

Thus Vergil found occasion to speak of rebellion, treason, war, good
government and bad, all of the matters that go to the making and un-
making of kingdoms, and he spoke as one who in the vicarious experience
of history had learned well the political lessons which are needful.

By way of contrast to Vergil's attack upon the reliability of Geoffrey
of Monmouth it is interesting to note the attitude of John Rastell in his
Pastime of People. Rastell seems to have doubted Geoffrey as much as
did Vergil, but he considered the end more important than the means.
Therefore, while acknowledging that he did not wish his readers precisely
to believe what he rehearsed out of Geoffrey, he proceeded with the story
as given by that author because he found there many examples of princes
who governed well,

> and also a man reding in the same shall see how the stroke of God fell ever
> uppon the people, other by battell, darth, or deth, for their vice and mis-
> leving; and also how divers princis and grete men, exaltid in pride and am-

---

[11] *Ibid.*, p. 139.   [12] *Ibid.*, pp. 189-90.

bicion, using tiranny and cruelte, or ells being neclygent in governyng of theyre people, or giffing them self to vicious liffing, were ever by the stroke of God punished for the same.[13]

That Henry VIII, like his father, took a personal interest in the writing of history is very evident. Lord Berners, translating Froissart at the king's command, as he tells us, added a preface in which he quoted Cicero, praised history as defying oblivion, being the best teacher, and constituting the only everlasting monument. Grynaeus, recommended by Erasmus, was given permission by the king to come to England to search for ancient monuments. But of far more importance was the appointment of John Leland to recover the antiquities of England, backed by the royal authority which was necessary. Holinshed records two Latin epigrams made in honor of the king and his bounty by Leland, who apparently was expected to offset the doubting Vergil.[14] We learn a good deal about the historian and his methods and purposes from the report which he made in 1546 to Henry VIII and which was published in 1549 with annotations and a new dedication to Edward VI by John Bale as *The Laboryouse Journey and Serche of Johan Leylande for Englands Antiquities*. Bale says that Leland prepared himself for his task:

as for all authors of Greke, Latyne, Frenche, Italian, Spanyshe, Bryttyshe, Saxonyshe, Walshe, Englyshe, or Scottyshe, towching in any wyse the understandynge of our Antiquitees, he had so fullye redde and applyed them, that they were in a maner graffed in hym as of nature. So that he myght well cal him selfe *Antiquarius*.[15]

Bale argued that want of access to the ancient records of Britain had caused Caxton, Fabyan, Hardyng, and now Vergil to err as they had in many points.

And .ii. thynges chefely have caused them (Leylande sayth) so longe to be witholden from us. The one is the slacknesse of empryntynge . . . An other is the want of ornature, that they have not bene changed into a more eloquent stile, to the full satisfyenge of delycate eares and wyttes.[16]

And we have the expansion of these ideas in Leland's own report that he had collected, both for the royal libraries and his own, ancient authors

---

[13] In the reprint by T. F. Dibdin (London, 1811), p. 7.
[14] He published his reply in 1544. *Assertio Inclytissimi Arturii Regis*. It was translated into English in 1582 by Richard Robinson.
[15] Fol. B5^r.　　　　　　　　　　[16] Fol. C3^v.

which had lain "secretely in corners" and remained unknown because
they were not printed, and because they had not been "clothed in purpure." Since we have in this latter reason Leland's recognition of the
claims of the humanist rhetoricians, his words are important:

> And also because men of eloquence hath not enterprised to set them fourth
> in a floryshynge style, in some tymes past not commenly used in Englande of
> writers, otherwise wele learned, and nowe in suche estymacyon, that except
> truth be delycately clothed in purpure her written verytes can scant fynde a
> reader.[17]

The works which Leland projected it is not here in point to recount
in detail; but it should be noted that he proposed to establish the antiquity and the originality of the English church, the claims of Englishmen
to greatness through the ages, the historical greatness of England, shire
by shire, and the true relation of England to ancient Rome. Most of the
proposed work he did not live to complete, but his records and papers
were used by many of the succeeding generation of historians.[18]

Bale was inclined to think the "purpure" of fine writing might be dispensed with, but he looked upon Leland's work as fulfilling the duty of
Englishmen both as Christians and as patriots to write history. He especially recommended histories to Christian governors as mirrors wherein
the cause and the reformation of abuses might be seen, and he linked
Biblical and secular history together in his praise.

Though he did not fail to repeat the usual humanistic arguments for
history, Bale stressed the Reformation special pleading: that the prophecies of the Bible will by history be understood, that the fallacies of
papistical teaching will be undermined, that the history of the English
church as well as of the English nation will be brought to light. And he
urged noblemen and rich merchants to pay for printing one by one
the works of antiquity. A single "belly banquet" foregone would pay for
the printing of three important works and would contribute to winning
new respect for England from France and Italy. Also he begged that there
be saved for posterity the great works left unfinished at the death of their
authors. In this connection he praised Thomas Cooper for completing

---

[17] Fol. C3ʳ (wrongly numbered C5).

[18] An early account of the peregrinations of Leland's papers is given in [William
Huddesford], *The Lives of those Eminent Antiquaries John Leland, Thomas Hearne,
and Anthony à Wood* (Oxford, 1772), I, 26-29. *The Laboryouse Journey* is reprinted
in this work also.

the work of Lanquet and the one who was responsible for printing the chronicle of Edward Halle.

But before I can continue the discussion of the work of the historians mentioned by Bale, I must return to the writer who along with Polydore Vergil is ranked highest by all historiographers. Sir Thomas More is important because he wrote *The History of Richard the Third* with such theatrical effectiveness that no one has yet been able to change or to qualify in the popular mind the picture which he presented of the usurping tyrant and his dreadful end. Fueter compares his work to that of the school of Leonardo Bruni (Aretine) in Italy . . . . He also notes critically his political bias . . . .

It was Roger Ascham who most truly saw the place of More in the history of English historical writing, for recalling his discussions about history with Sir Robert Asteley, and questioning the *what* and the *why* and the *how* of history, he formulated as clearly as anyone in England basic standards of judgment. When he wrote of More to Asteley, he judged him by these careful standards:

> Syr Thomas More in that pamphlet of Richard the thyrd, doth in most part I beleve of all these pointes so content men, as if the rest of our story of England were so done, we might well compare with Fraunce, Italy, or Germany in that behalfe.

The points he set out are in reality an outline of humanistic theory and are so important that, though I am keeping Ascham's words, I am separating them from their enveloping text for emphasis:

(1) to write nothyng false,
(2) to be bold to say any truth,
(3) to marke diligently the causes, counsels, actes and issues in all great attemptes,
(4) of euery issue, to note some generall lesson of wisedome and warines, for lyke matters in time to come,
(5) [to use diligence] to kepyng truly the order of tyme,
(6) [to describe] lyvely, both the site of places and the nature of persons not onely for the outward shape of the body: but also for the inward disposition of the mynde.

And Ascham added concerning the appropriate style:

> The stile must be alwayes playne and open: yet sometime higher and lower as matters do ryse and fall: for if proper and naturall wordes, in well joyned

sentences do lyvely expresse the matter, be it troublesome, quyet, angry or pleasant, a man shal thinck not to be readyng but present in doyng of the same.[19]

More's adherence to the truth and the time order is not of so much interest here as is his realizing of the other ideals set down by Ascham. He did record, not merely deeds, but also all the causes, counsels, acts, and issues from which they resulted; his long analysis of Richard's choice of exactly the right moment to seize the crown is a case in point.[20] His history is full of general lessons "for lyke matters in time to come." Thus, after describing Richard's coronation, he moralizes: "And as the thing evil got is never well kept, through all the time of his reign never ceased there cruel death and slaughter, till his own destruction ended it." And after telling of the murder of the two little princes, he comments that "God never gave this world a more notable example, neither in what unsurety standeth this worldly weal, or what mischief worketh the proud enterprises of an high heart, or finally, what wretched end ensueth such dispiteous cruelty."

He described the physical appearance of his characters so that they could walk on the stage, and the "inward disposition of the mind" so vividly that it could be dramatized. I quote one brief passage by way of illustration, the passage describing Richard after the murder of the princes:

> For I have heard by credible report, of such as were secret with his chamberers, that after this abominable deed done, he never had quiet in his mind, he never thought himself sure: where he went abroad, his eyes whirled about, his body privily fenced, his hand ever on his dagger, his countenance and manner like one always ready to strike again; he took ill rest o' nights, lay long waking and musing, sore wearied with care and watch, rather slumbered than slept, troubled with fearful dreams, suddenly sometime started up, leaped out of his bed and ran about the chamber, so was his restless heart continually tossed and tumbled with the tedious impression and stormy remembrance of his abominable deed.[21]

Furthermore, like Thucydides, he made his characters speak real speeches as though recorded by a stenographer at the time. This habit, too,

---

[19] "R. Ascham to John Asteley" prefixed to Ascham's *Report and Discourse . . . of the Affaires and State of Germany* (London, 1570?). Written in response to a letter from Asteley dated October, 1552.

[20] Sir Thomas More, *The English Works,* ed. W. E. Campbell (London and New York, 1927-1931), I, 433.

[21] *Ibid.,* pp. 451-52.

contributed to the dramatic quality of the writing and made the transition from narrative to dramatic presentation easier.

The effect of More's *Richard* upon the chronicles which we have specially to consider as the sources of Shakespeare's historical plays can scarcely be overestimated. As is well known, it was first published with Hardyng's *Chronicle* in 1543 as a part of the extension by Richard Grafton derived from "diverse and sondry autours that have writen of the affaires of Englande." [22] Grafton finished out the story of Richard in the same general style that More had used. But Grafton showed the influence of the Reformation in putting in God as more conspicuously the stage manager of the worldly events he recorded. More wrote like a humanist, though like a Christian humanist. Grafton wrote like a Reformation humanist.

More's work was printed for the second time though still with certain inaccuracies in the chronicle of Edward Halle, posthumously issued by Richard Grafton in 1548,[23] and it lived on in the succeeding chronicles which built one upon another.

Halle's history is organized about the lives and reigns of eight kings, seen in the table of contents:

An introduction into the devision of the two houses of Lancastre and Yorke.
    i. The unquiet tyme of kyng Henry the fowerth,
    ii. The victorious actes of kyng Henry the v.
   iii. The troubleous season of kyng Henry the vi.
  iiii. The prosperous reigne of kyng Edward the iiii.
    v. The pitifull life of kyng Edward the v.
   vi. The tragicall doynges of kyng Richard the iii.
  vii. The politike goveraunce of kyng Henry the vii.
 viii. The triumphant reigne of king Henry the viii.

His chronicle was undoubtedly written to serve the political purposes of Henry VIII, being directed to teaching political lessons in general and one imperative lesson in particular, the destruction that follows rebellion and civil dissension in a realm. Dr. W. Gordon Zeeveld would, indeed, place it as the most ambitious of the inspired works of propaganda of the first

[22] The collations of the various texts of More's history are to be found in the Campbell edition, the work of W. A. G. Doyle-Davidson, pp. 229-317. R. W. Chambers in an essay on "The Authorship of the 'History of Richard III' " (pp. 24-53) gives an account of the publication of the various editions.

[23] Concerning the supposed 1542 edition of Halle's work and the general history of the publishing of the chronicle, see A. F. Pollard, "Edward Hall's Will and Chronicle," in the *Bulletin of the Institute for Historical Research,* IX (1932), 171-77.

half of the sixteenth century, "whose purpose was to scotch such dormant subversive elements in the kingdom as dared to raise their heads." [24] The very title of Halle's work is political:

> The Union of the Two Noble and Illustre Famelies of Lancastre and Yorke, beeyng long in continual discension for the croune of this noble realme, with all the actes done in bothe the tymes of the Princes, bothe of the one linage and of the other, beginnyng at the tyme of kyng Henry the fowerth, the first aucthor of this devision, and so successively proceadyng to the reigne of the high and prudent prince kyng Henry the eight, the undubitate flower and very heir of both the sayd linages.

His theme is sounded in the opening passage:

> What mischiefe hath insurged in realmes by intestine devision, what depopulacion hath ensued in countries my civill discencion, what detestable murder hath been committed in citees by seperate faccions, and what calamitee hath ensued in famous regions by domestical discord and unnaturall controversy: Rome hath felt, Italy can testifie, Fraunce can bere witnes, Beame can tell, Scotlande maie write, Denmarke can shewe, and especially this noble realme of Englande can apparantly declare and make demonstracion.

And as he speaks of the particular horror of the wars caused by the dissension between the houses of York and Lancaster, he adds pertinently:

> For what noble man liveth at this date, or what gentleman of any auncient stocke or progeny is clere, whose linage hath not ben infested and plaged with this unnaturall devision.

Halle's dedication of his work to the king showed him a master of the familiar humanistic doctrines concerning history, as do the many stock-in-trade defenses of history or historical method scattered throughout his work. He quoted Cicero when he once more defined history as "the witnesses of tymes, the light of trueth, and the life of memory." [25] He saw history as the only means of fighting "the cancard enemie," "the suckyng serpent," "the dedly darte," "the defacer"—Oblivion.[26] Only Gildas and Geoffrey of Monmouth had rescued England's ancient history, and after Froissart, who ended his history at the beginning of the reign of Henry IV, Halle says, no one but Fabyan and "one without name, which

---

[24] "Richard Morison, Official Apologist for Henry VIII," *PMLA*, LV (1940), 413 and note 52.

[25] Fols. ccli and cclii of the section on Henry VIII.

[26] In the dedication to Edward VI.

wrote the common English Chronicle," had written in the English lan-
gauge of the seven kings who followed Richard II. Of these two later
writers he comments that they were "men worthy to be praysed for their
diligence, but farre shotyng wide from the butte of an historie."

With complete disregard of the anachronism involved in his doing
so, the ghost of the Earl of Worcester is made to comment in the *Mirror
for Magistrates* upon the relative merits of Fabyan and Halle, showing
what "the butte of an historie" should be:

> Unfruytfull Fabyan folowed the face
> Of time and dedes, but let the causes slip:
> Whych Hall hath added, but with double grace,
> For feare I think least trouble might him trip: . . .[27]

The same prophetic ghost forecast the banning of Halle's work.

In the history of sixteenth-century history writing in England, Halle
is actually of great importance for three reasons. First, though he is
proved by modern scholars to have incorporated in his work many facts
and views taken from Vergil, often merely acting as translator,[28] he was
still the first of the sixteenth century writers to write in English in the
fashion of the Renaissance a history of England covering a considerable
period of time. Like Vergil, whose work he used, and like More, whose
Richard III he incorporated as a whole in his chronicle, he described the
physical appearance of men and places, he analyzed psychological conflicts and their issues, he probed for the causes of events, he emphasized
the end of the action and the manner of a man's death as revealing the
judgment finally imposed in a moral universe.

Second, he wrote with an avowed political aim, and like both Vergil
and More, he made the lessons drawn from history both explicit and
capable of general application. Pre-eminent, as I have said, was the lesson
of the danger to a nation when civil discord and rebellion were allowed
to raise their ugly heads.

Finally, and of special interest in this study, Halle presented a period
of English history, from the beginning of the trouble between Richard II
and Henry Bolingbroke to the end of the conflict between the houses of
York and Lancaster, which was to be the period most dealt with in the
literature of the time. The *Mirror for Magistrates* was confessedly based
primarily upon Halle, and it moralized his history into its many tragedies.
Daniel dealt with this period in his *Civil Wars*, and there were many

---

[27] *The Mirror for Magistrates,* ed. L. B. Campbell (Cambridge, 1938), p. 198.
[28] See note 7 above.

dramas and poems written about it, because its lessons were pertinent in Tudor times. But above all, Shakespeare chose to write his greatest historical plays about this period, and he opened his *Richard II* at the exact point at which Halle begins his history. Because of the way in which one of the English chroniclers incorporated the work of another, only to be himself used by the next, it is impossible to distinguish the indebtedness of poets and dramatists to specific historians, but the debt of literary men of the English Renaissance to Halle was very great.

It was Richard Grafton, famous above all for the large part he played in making the Bible in English accessible to his countrymen, who incorporated More's life of Richard III in his extension of Hardyng's chronicle and printed both works for the first time. It was Grafton who published Halle's chronicle after the author's death. Quite logically a man who had salvaged so much historical writing began to compile from "sundry authors" his own account of English history. A preliminary work was published in 1562 with the title of *An Abridgement of the Chronicles of England,* and it was dedicated to Lord Robert Dudley, afterward the Earl of Leicester, as one who had prepared himself for a part in government by reading histories. Grafton recited to his patron the traditional praises of history, reaching his climax with the Reformation addition: "But the principall commoditie in the highest respecte is the settynge foorth of the course of Godds doinges."

This preliminary chronicle was followed in 1565 by *A Manuell of the Chronicles of England* and in 1568 and 1569 by his great work,[29] the two-volume history of the world which served to orient England's history, as is indicated in the title:

A Chronicle at Large and Meere History of the Affayres of England and Kinges of the Same, deduced from the creation of the worlde, unto the first habitation of this islande: and so by contynuance unto the first yere of the reigne of our most deere and sovereigne lady Queene Elizabeth: collected out of sundry aucthours, whose names are expressed in the next page.

The dedication to Cecil includes interesting criticism of historical writing in England:

For among so many writers, there hath yet none to my knowledge, published any full, playne and meere Englishe historie. For some of them of purpose meaning to write short notes in maner of Annales, commonly called Abridge-

---

[29] The second volume is dated 1568, the first 1569. It is probable that the STC 12146 is not a separate edition of the whole work but the first edition of the second volume.

says Holinshed, "was politicly handled," "secretly kept" and his purpose "ready" before it was "openly published" (*Hol.*, p. 212; *Stone*, p. 255). If all that York stands for in history is to be properly conveyed in the play, his emergence when "mischief breaks out" must take his enemies by surprise. But it must not take the audience by surprise; hence Shakespeare introduces short conspiratorial scenes to put fellow Yorkists *partly* "in the know" (the colloquialism fits the mood), and adds a number of soliloquies to put the audience wholly in the know. The soliloquy given to York at *Part 2* (I. i. 209) becomes the first experiment in the form to be turned to such advantage in *Richard III*; it enlists the audience's sympathy against the "others," exploits its readiness to take a low view of human nature and be brutally realistic about politics. In this first soliloquy York voices the muscular chronicle judgment that critics have sometimes taken for Shakespeare's definitive verdict on Henry:

> And force perforce I'll make him yield the crown.
> Whose bookish rule hath pull'd fair England down.
>
> [Pt. 2, I. i. 253]

But the rough verbal shoulder-shrugging of York is precisely expressive of the factious energy which does most to pull down fair England. A second soliloquy, in the same manner, sets York, "the labouring spider," behind the inception of the Cade rebellion (Pt. 2, V. i. 1).

In a passage of reflection on "the tragicall state of this land under the rent regiment of King Henrie," Holinshed speaks of the "sundrie practices" which "imbecilled" the "prerogative" of the King, and wonders at the pitched battles, which he divides into two groups, that were fought over and about him (*Hol.*, p. 272-3). Shakespeare keeps the outline and emphasizes the distinction between the military and political sources of catastrophe. The first two acts deal with the battles of 1460-61, when Henry had that "naked name of king"; the third and fourth acts are dominantly political, and about the chicanery of the nobles with their rival kings; and the last presents the campaigns of 1471, in which politics and war are indistinguishable. Once again one is struck in performance by the expressive force of the mere dumb-show and noise (witness the stage directions); kings and crowns are treated as stage properties to enforce the chronicle moral about contempt for sovereignty, and Warwick is made quite literally the setter-up and plucker-down of kings (e.g. IV. iii). The pantomime is as skilful in the political scenes. The scene in the French court (III. iii), for instance, where Margaret has won the support of King Lewis, only to lose it to Warwick who comes as ambassador from Edward, becomes a superb exercise in the acrobatics of diplomacy, when letters are at last brought from Edward about the Bona marriage.

For the greater part of the third play Shakespeare is content to follow Holinshed in making his characters public masks, without intimately felt life, and therefore hardly seeming responsible for what they do. He tightens the sequence of atrocities, telescopes time, and eliminates all rituals of government, until the stage action and reaction appear yet more savagely mechanical than in the chronicle. So long as the characterization is neutral the first tetralogy displays a barbarous providence ruling murderous automatons whose reactions are predictable in terms of certain quasi-Hobbesian assumptions about human nature: when argument fails men resort to force; when an oath is inconvenient they break it; their power challenged, they retort with violence; their power subdued they resort to lies, murder or suicide; their honour impugned, they look for revenge; their enemies at their mercy, they torture and kill them; and if a clash of loyalties occurs they resolve it in the interest of their own survival. Such might be the vision of the play's pantomime, but its dimensions are not confined to its pantomime and to its shallower rhetoric. The anarchic, egocentric impulses are not presented as the inescapable laws of human nature; they are at most manifestations of forces that automatically take over when the constraints of government are withheld. Law and order cease to prevail when men cease to believe in them, and the process by which this comes about is explored in the play's dominant characters.

The figures of Clifford and York who, in *Part 2*, personalize two kinds of anarchic scepticism—the soldier's nihilism and the politician's realism —are displaced in *Part 3* by the more significant contrast between Richard of Gloster and King Henry. With obvious propriety these are chosen to characterize the moral tensions which give meaning to the deep chaos of the last phase of the reign. But the crimes of the Roses Wars are so multiple and their agents so numerous, that Shakespeare could not attempt, even if at this early date it were within his power, the comprehensively intimate exploration of evil he undertakes in *Macbeth,* and he allows himself only that measure of intimate soliloquy and address which will accord with the conventions of historical pageant.

In the first two plays the chronicle myth of a King absurdly and irrelevantly virtuous can just about pass muster, and in the first scene of *Part 3,* Henry's virtue is still associated with impotence; his war of "frowns, words, and threats" is disarmed by his readiness to concede the Yorkist claims, by the wry defection of Exeter (unwarranted by the history), and by the Robin Hood trickery of Warwick; his conscience-stricken asides carry as little conviction as his military posturing, and one feels the *gaucherie* is the playwright's as well as the character's. In the next phase, however, Shakespeare's tragic art wins distinction from the ferocity of the material and Henry assumes a stature outside the chronicle compass.

Both the finer qualities of Henry's virtue and the intensity of Richard of Gloster's virulence spring from Shakespeare's treatment of the Battle of Wakefield. Conventional heroic ideals cannot survive the battle which turns on two blasphemies of chivalry—the killing of the prince and the degradation of the mock-king. Clifford's slaughter of Rutland (I. iii), in calculated contempt of the Priest and the law of arms, is a repudiation of the myth that expects from every "gentleman" in battle the virtues of the lion. The values apt to an heroic battle play are displaced by those prevailing in parts of English Seneca; in Heywood's *Thyestes,* for example, where "ire thinks nought unlawful to be done," "Babes be murdered ill" and "bloodshed lies the land about" (I. i. 79-89). Shakespeare gives the revenge motive a great political significance by relating it to the dynastic feud for which Clifford is not alone responsible.

Anarchism, Shakespeare had learned from the Cade scenes, is more dramatic when it is iconoclastic, and the next Wakefield outrage, the paper crowning (I. iv), mutilates the idols of Knighthood, Kingship, Womanhood and Fatherhood. In making a ritual of the atrocity Shakespeare imitates the history—the scene is a formal set-piece because it was so staged by its historical performers. Holinshed tells how the Lancastrians made obeisance and cried, "Haile, king without rule"—"as the Jewes did unto Christ" (*Hol.* p. 269; *Stone,* p. 299). Although Shakespeare suppresses the open blasphemy, he keeps the crucifixion parallel with the line, "Now looks he like a King" (I. iv. 96), and, more significantly, by combining the mockery reported in one of a choice of chronicle accounts with the paper-coronation in another (*Hol.,* p. 268; *Stone,* p. 299). He takes little liberty with the chronicle, moreover, when he makes the stage-managed historical ceremony into an ordered, antiphonal combat of words, with Northumberland presiding, as it were, in the rhetorical lists. In spite of the controlling formality the language moves on several planes between gnomic generalization, " 'Tis government that makes them seem divine, The want thereof makes thee abominable" (I. iv. 132); stylized feeling, "Oh tiger's heart wraps in a woman's hide! How could'st thou drain the life-blood of the child" (I. iv. 137); plain, personal pathos, "This cloth thou dip'dst in blood of my sweet boy" (I. iv. 157); and colloquial venom, "And where's that valiant crook-back prodigy, Dicky, your boy, that with his grumbling voice Was wont to cheer his dad in mutinies?" In the blinding scene of *King Lear* the same changes will be rung in a richer peal, but there is enough in the Wakefield scene's counterpoint of reflection and feeling to tax the resources of its actors.

Henry is not made witness to the event. He is allowed the dignity of total isolation, and when he comes to the stage molehill at Towton (II. v), it is to speak the most moving of Shakespeare's comments on the civil wars. Shakespeare is less fully engaged when he writes about the objectives of the battle as seen by the participants than by its futility as it appears to a suffering observer. Hall had felt a similar need to withdraw into reflection:

> This conflict was in maner unnaturall, for in it the sonne fought agaynst the father, the brother agaynst the brother, the Nephew agaynst the Uncle, and the tenaunt agaynst hys Lorde, which slaughter did sore and much weaken the puyssance of this realme. (1548/1809, p. 256)

In *Gorboduc* and in Daniel's *Civil Wars* the commonplace is retailed with a complacent omniscience damaging to living language.[3] But by attributing it to the King in the course of battle Shakespeare is able to quicken it with personal feeling; beneath the ceremonious surface we again sense the pulse and surge of events.

The hint for the opening lines is one of Hall's "ebb and flow of battle" clichés (*Stone*, p. 306), but Shakespeare insinuates rarer images of the peaceful, symmetrical rhythms of nature—"the morning's war" and "the shepheard blowing of his nails," and after touching the conflicts inherent in nature, arrests the movement of battle in that of the sea—"the equal poise of this fell war." A glance at the humour and pathos of Henry's isolation (Margaret and Clifford have chid him from the battle), with a touch of wry exhaustion ("Would I were dead, if God's good will were so"), offers assurance of Shakespeare's gift for "re-living the past," and the sequent lines of exquisite pastoral seem to re-create the convention out of the kind of human experience which underlies it. An alarum returns us to the battle and to a glimpse of its victims in another statuesque mirror-scene in which blood and pallor are made heraldic (II. v. 97 ff.). Once again the feeling for the past is the cathedral-pavement sort, not the chronicle sort; it is at once a refreshing and a potentially devitalizing mood, and after a hundred and twenty lines Shakespeare pulls us out of it and lets the pantomime get under way again.

The authority of Henry's commentary on Towton is sufficiently memorable to help vindicate the innocence of the speech he makes before

---

[3] The peroration of *Gorboduc* and the first stanza of *The Civil Wars*.

the keepers arrest him: "My pity hath been balm to heal their wounds. My mildness hath allay'd their swelling griefs, My mercy dry'd their water-flowing tears" (IV. viii. 41 ff.). From this and a few other passages in the plays it would be possible to present Henry as the centre of a moral parable whose lineaments are traced in Thomas Elyot's *The Governour*. The King, says Elyot, must be merciful, but too much *Clementia* is a sickness of mind; as soon as any offend him the King should "immediately strike him with his most terrible dart of vengeance." But the occasions when Henry seems guilty of an excess of virtue are rare, and he is at his most impressive when he is martyred in his last scene of *Part 3*, not when he tries to throw his weight about in the first. The Wakefield battle once fought, moreover, "the terrible dart of vengeance" is lost to the armoury of virtue. Henry's bemused and disappointed faith in the political efficacy of mercy, pity, peace and love does not deserve the editorial mockery it has received—"characteristically effeminate" and "smug complacency." [4] Henry's virtue may be defective but Shakespeare commands from his audience a full reverence for it when, at the moment of his extermination, the King confronts his ultimate antagonist, Richard of Gloster.

Richard is introduced as York's heroic soldier son, but in his first characteristic speech of length (II. i. 79 ff.) he becomes the bitter, unchivalrous avenger—a reaction to the Messenger's report of Wakefield which seems instinctive and inevitable. But Richard not only reacts to events (all the barons do that) he also becomes the conscious embodiment of all the drives—moral, intellectual and physical—that elsewhere show themselves only in the puppetry. Translating into theatrical terms, we might say that when he takes the stage for his first exercise of the soliloquy-prerogative he inherits from York (at the end of III. ii), his language shows him capable of playing the parts of York, Clifford, Edward, Margaret or Warwick. All their energies are made articulate: the doggedness of York "that reaches at the moon" and the same eye for the glitter of the Marlovian crown; the dedication to evil which characterizes Clifford; the prurience of Edward; the decorated and ruthless rhetoric of Margaret; and Warwick's gifts of king-maker, resolute "to command, to check, to overbear." Shakespeare has him use the fantastic lore about his birth to admirable effect: it strengthens the impression of blasphemy against love and fertility, makes deformity license depravity and, most important, allegorizes the birth of a political monster in the present by recalling that of a physical monster in the past, "like to a chaos or an unlick'd bear-whelp." But it is not all specifically birth-imagery—about Richard having teeth and the dogs howling. The sense of violent struggle, of

---

[4] See notes to IV. viii. 38-50 in Hart's Arden and Wilson's New Cambridge Editions.

unnatural energies breaking free, is best caught in lines that are not
explicitly about birth at all:

> And I—like one lost in a thorny wood,
> That rends the thorns and is rent with the thorns,
> Seeking a way and straying from the way;
> Not knowing how to find the open air,
> But toiling desperately to find it out—
> Torment myself to catch the English crown:
> And from that torment I will free myself,
> Or hew my way out with a bloody axe.
>
> [III. ii. 174]

It is from the kennel of England's womb that this hell-hound is to bite
itself free. At the end of the soliloquy Richard promises the audience a
performance more entertaining than any heroic fantasy or medieval
Trojan legend; he will outplay all politic dissemblers, "add colours to
the camelion," "change shapes with Proteus" and "set the *murtherous*
Machivill to school." The ground is prepared for *Richard III*, where for
three acts the comic idiom will dominate the tragic, with politics a
kings' game best played by cunning actors.

But the continuity with the mood of *Richard III* is deliberately frac-
tured and the tragic mode made to dominate the comic in the scene of
Henry's death. The King opposes Richard's tongue and sword with a
moral force that Shakespeare makes all but transcendent and the "scene
of death" that "Roscius"—the actor and devil Richard—performs at last,
comes near to a tragic consummation. Yet the qualifications "all but" and
"comes near" are, after all, necessary. The brute facts of history will not
allow a satisfying tragic outcome; Shakespeare cannot pretend that the
martyrdom of an innocent king appeased the appetite of providence or
exhausted the sophisticated savagery that Richard stands for.

Nor can Hall's dynastic myth be enlisted to reassure us that all will be
well when the White Rose is wedded to the Red—that will only be
possible at the end of *Richard III* when, in a kind of postscript to the
complete tetralogy, Richmond will step into the Elizabethan present and
address an audience sufficiently remote from Henry's reign. As it is, the
plays of *Henry VI* are not, as it were, haunted by the ghost of Richard II,
and the catastrophes of the civil wars are not laid to Bolingbroke's charge;
the catastrophic virtue of Henry and the catastrophic evil of Richard are
not an inescapable inheritance from the distant past but are generated
by the happenings we are made to witness.

The questioning of the ways of God and the roles of good and evil in

English history will be re-opened in *Richard III,* but in the interim *Part 3* ends, as tragedies remotely derived from fertility rites of course should, with some elaborate imagery of autumn reaping. It is fitting that Richard should be standing by to blast the harvest and to boast himself a Judas.

Note

First Editions. A "bad" quarto (1594) and a "bad" octavo (1595) bear, respectively, the titles: "The first part of the Contention betwixt the two famous Houses of Yorke and Lancaster . . . with the notable Rebellion of Jacke Cade: and the Duke of Yorkes first claime unto the Crowne" and "The true Tragedie of Richard Duke of Yorke, and the death of good King Henrie the Sixt, with the whole contention betweene the two Houses Lancaster and Yorke, as it was sundrie times enacted by the Right Honourable the Earle of Pembrooke his Servants." As Greg remarks in *The Shakespeare First Folio* (1955) "the two parts of *The Contention between the Houses of York and Lancaster"* are too closely connected to have different histories, though "their relation to 2 and 3 *Henry VI* has been a standing problem of Shakespearian criticism"; *1, 2* and *3 Henry VI* are Folio (1623) texts.

Modern Editions. The authoritative modern edition of *1, 2* and *3 Henry VI* is the New Cambridge Shakespeare, edited by J. Dover Wilson (3 vols., 1952), who has strong views on the authorship question. There is a New Arden Edition of *2 Henry VI* (1956) edited by A. S. Cairncross with a useful and comprehensive introduction. W. W. Greg has edited *The True Tragedy of Richard Duke of York, 1595* (Shakespeare Quarto Facsimiles, 1958).

Scholarship and Criticism. Extracts from the substantial source material of *1, 2* and *3 Henry VI* are provided in G. Bullough's *Narrative and Dramatic Sources of Shakespeare,* Vol. III (1960). W. G. Boswell-Stone edited Holinshed's *Chronicle* as *Shakespeare's Holinshed* (1896); this edition is referred to [above] as *Stone,* and references simply to *Hol.* are to the reprint (1808) of the 1587 edition of Holinshed. L. B. Campbell's *Shakespeare's Histories* (1947) and E. M. W. Tillyard's *Shakespeare's History Plays* are referred to by their authors' names. J. P. Brockbank holds that Dover Wilson's arguments concerning authorship of the *Henry VI* plays can be refuted; that the plays were written in their Folio order (which is strongly suggested by the equable division of the source material); that Shakespeare was wholly responsible for them and that the oddities and incoherences in the text cannot be explained by a collaboration theory; that Robert Greene's jealousy of Shakespeare may be accounted for if we postulate his authorship of an early popular play on Henry V (perhaps the original of the *Famous Victories*); and that Shakespeare's plays of Henry VI were the first to engage closely and responsibly with chronicle material.

Stage-History. The New Cambridge Edition provides a stage-history. In *Shakespeare Survey* (1953) Sir Barry Jackson writes "On producing *Henry VI"* with reference to his Birmingham Repertory Theatre production, by Douglas Seale, of *2* and *3 Henry VI* in 1952. This company performed the trilogy at the Old Vic Theatre in 1953.

Angel with Horns:
The Unity of *Richard III*

by A. P. Rossiter

"Let's write 'good angel' on the devil's horn"
—*Measure for Measure, II,* iv. 16

In the Second Part of *Henry IV* (III. i.) the King and Warwick are talking away the midnight, or the King's insomnia; and the King remembers how Richard spoke like a prophet of the future treachery of the Percies. Warwick replies that those who look for rotations in history can indeed appear to be prophets:

> There is a history in all men's lives,
> Figuring the nature of the times deceas'd;
> The which observ'd, a man may prophesy,
> With a near aim, of the main chance of things
> As yet not come to life, who in their seeds
> And weak beginnings lie intreasured.
> Such things become the hatch and brood of time.

Richard, he explains, had observed "the necessary form" of the events he had seen happen; and from that he could "create a perfect guess" of some that were to ensue as "the hatch and brood of time."

Men have always looked for such a predictability in history: it gives the illusion of a comfortably ordered world. They have also often read—and written—historical records to show that the course of events has been guided by a simple process of divine justice, dispensing rewards and pun-

"Angel with Horns: The Unity of *Richard III*." From *Angel with Horns* (London: Longmans, Green & Co. Ltd., 1961), by A. P. Rossiter, pp. 1-22. Copyright © 1961 by Longmans, Green & Co. Ltd. Reprinted by permission of Theatre Arts Books, New York, N.Y. and Longmans, Green & Co. Ltd. This lecture was originally given in 1953 to the Shakespeare Summer School at Stratford-upon-Avon.

ishments here on earth and seeing to it that the wicked do *not* thrive like the green bay-tree (as the Psalmist thought), and that virtue is not "triumphant only in theatrical performances" (as the humane Mikado put it: being a Gilbertian Japanese, not an Elizabethan Christian). The story-matter of the Henry VI plays and of *Richard III* accepted both of these comforting and comfortable principles.

When I say "story-matter" I mean what the Chronicles gave the author (or authors) of these four plays, and I wish to remain uncommitted as to whether their *plots* (and especially that of *Richard III*) work entirely within those reassuring limitations.

I am averse to source-study, as material for lectures. Yet sad experience of human nature (and perhaps of historians) leads me to remind you how the Richard III myth *("story")* came to reach Shakespeare. In the play, you remember, the Bishop of Ely, Morton, plots with Buckingham and runs away to join Richmond (Henry Tudor). He duly became one of Henry's ministers; and Thomas More grew up in his household—and later wrote the life of Richard III. It would only be human if Morton recounted all the worst that was ever said of the master he had betrayed: it is not surprising that Edward Halle should accept More's account, in writing his vast book on the "noble and illustre families of Lancastre and York"; and still more human that Raphael Holinshed (whom no one could call a historian) should copy extensively from Halle—and so leave room for all those since Horace Walpole who have had doubts about the historical character of this terrible monarch and the events of his times.

To think that we are seeing anything like sober history in this play is derisible naïvety. What we are offered is a formally patterned sequence presenting two things: on the one hand, a rigid Tudor *schema* of retributive justice (a sort of analogy to Newton's Third Law in the field of moral dynamics: "Action and reaction are equal and apposite"); and, on the other, a huge triumphant stage-personality, an early old masterpiece of the art of rhetorical stage-writing, a monstrous being incredible in any sober, historical scheme of things—Richard himself.

I will talk about the first, first. The basic pattern of retributive justice (or God's vengeance) is well enough illustrated in Holinshed, in the passage telling how Prince Edward (Henry VI's son and Margaret's) was murdered at the Battle of Tewkesbury. The Prince was handed over to Edward IV on the proclamation of a promise that he would not be harmed; he was brought before the King, asked why he "durst so presumptuously enter into his realm" and replied courageously "To recover my father's kingdom and heritage" (and more to that purpose)—but let Holinshed say the rest:

At which words king Edward said nothing, but with his hand thrust him from him, or (as some saie) stroke him with his gantlet; whom incontinentlie, George duke of Clarence, Richard duke of Glocester, Thomas Greie marquesse Dorcet, and William lord Hastings, that stood by, suddenlie murthered; for the which cruell act, the more part of the dooers in their latter daies dranke of the like cup, by the righteous iustice and due punishment of God.

There you have the notional pattern, in little, of the whole framework of *Richard III:* Clarence—"false, fleeting, perjur'd Clarence" (who took the sacrament to remain true to Henry VI of Lancaster and deserted him); Gray—one of the group of Queen Elizabeth Woodeville's relations, who fall to Richard and Buckingham next after Clarence; Hastings, who says he will see "this crown of mine hewn from its shoulders/Before I see the crown so foul misplaced" (on Richard's head)—and *does* (if a man can be said to see his own decapitation). Holinshed really understates the matter in writing "the more part of the dooers . . . dranke of the like cup"; for of those he names, everyone did. On the one hand, that is what *Richard III* is about: what it is composed of. A heavy-handed justice commends the ingredients of a poisoned [cup].

This notional pattern of historic events rigidly determined by a mechanical necessity is partly paralleled by, partly modified by, the formal patterns of the episodes (or scenes) and the language. By "formal patterns" I mean the unmistakably iterated goings-on in scenes so exactly parallel that if the first *is* passable on a modern stage as quasi-realistic costume-play stuff, the second (repeating it always *more* unrealistically) cannot be. The two wooing-scenes (Richard with Anne and Elizabeth) are the simplest case; but in the lamentation-scenes—where a collection of bereft females comes together and goes through a dismal catalogue of *Who was Who* and *Who has lost Whom* (like a gathering of historical Mrs. Gummidges, each "thinking of the old 'un" with shattering simultaneity) —there, even editors have found the proceedings absurd; and readers difficult. When Queen Margaret, for example, says:

> I had an Edward, till a Richard kill'd him;
> I had a husband, till a Richard kill'd him:
> Thou hadst an Edward, till a Richard kill'd him;
> Thou hadst a Richard, till a Richard kill'd him,

[IV. iv. 40-43]

a reader may *just* keep up (and realize that the last two are the Princes in the Tower, so that Queen Elizabeth is being addressed); but when the Duchess of York takes up with

> I had a Richard too, and thou didst kill him;
> I had a Rutland too, thou holp'st to kill him,

it is likely that you are lost, unless your recollection of a *Henry VI* and the ends of Richard, Duke of York and his young son (Edmund) is unusually clear.

It is not only the iteration of scene that is stylized: the stiffly formal manipulation of echoing phrase and sequence of words within the scenes is even more unrealistic. A closely related parallelism exists in the repeated occurrence of a sort of "single line traffic" in sentences: the classicist's *stichomythia*. One speaker takes from the other exactly the same ration of syllables, and rejoins as if under contract to repeat the form of the given sentence as exactly as possible, using the maximum number of the same words or their logical opposites, or (failing that) words closely associated with them. I describe the game pedantically, because it *is* an exact and scientific game with language, and one of the graces and beauties of the play Shakespeare wrote. If we cannot accept the "patterned speech" of *Richard III*, its quality must remain unknown to us. "Early work" is an evasive, criticism-dodging term. Early it may be; but the play is a triumphant contrivance in a manner which cannot properly be compared with that of any other tragedy—nor of any history, except *3 Henry VI* (where the manner takes shape, and particularly in III. ii.) and *King John* (which is not half so well built or integrated as this).

I have emphasized the stylization of verbal patterning (with its neatly over-exact adjustments of stroke to stroke, as in royal tennis), because the sequence of most of the important events offers very much the same pattern. I might remark, in passing, that these verbal devices were offering to the Elizabethans an accomplished English equivalent to the neat dexterities they admired in Seneca (a point made by T. S. Eliot years ago; though he did not examine how the dramatic ironies of the action run in parallel with these counter-stroke reversals of verbal meaning, and form a kind of harmony). But we miss something more than Shakespeare's rhetorical game of tennis if merely irritated by, e.g.:

> *Anne:*   I would I knew thy heart.
> *Richard:* 'Tis figured in my tongue.
> *Anne:*   I fear me, both are false.
> *Richard:* Then never man was true.

Those reversals of intention (*heart-tongue; false-true*) are on precisely the pattern of the repeated reversals of human expectation, the reversals of events, the anticipated reversals (foreseen only by the audience), which make "dramatic irony." The patterned speech of the dialogue—the wit that demonstrates that a sentence is but a cheveril glove, quickly turned the other way—is fundamentally one with the ironic patterns of the plot. "Dramatic irony" here is verbal *peripeteia*.

You will see that simply exemplified if you read Buckingham's speech at the beginning of Act II, where he calls a curse on himself if ever he goes back on his reconciliation with the Queen (and is quite specific about it); then turn straight to his last lines in v. i., when he is on the way to execution: "That high All-seer, which I dallied with." He has got exactly what he asked for. He did not mean the words he used, but they have been reversed into actuality, in exactly the same way as verbal terms are reversed in the tennis-court game of rhetoric.

The same irony plays all over *Richard III*. It lurks like a shadow behind the naïvely self-confident Hastings; it hovers a moment over Buckingham when Margaret warns him against "yonder dog" (Richard), and, on Richard's asking what she said, he replies, "Nothing that I respect, my gracious lord" (1. iii. 296)—and this at a time when Buckingham is under no threat whatsoever.

Its cumulative effect is to present the personages as existing in a state of total and terrible uncertainty. This is enhanced if we know the details of what comes into the play from *3 Henry VI*, but is there even if we know only a few bare essentials of what has gone before. We need to know who Margaret is; how Lancaster has been utterly defeated, and King Henry and his son murdered; how Clarence betrayed his King and returned to the Yorkists; and how Richard, his younger brother, has already marked him as his immediate obstruction on his intended way to the crown. We need to know too that the Duchess of York is mother to that unrewarding trio, Edward IV, Clarence, Gloucester; that Edward IV has married an aspiring commoner, Elizabeth Grey (*née* Woodeville); and that she has jacked up her relations into nobility. Beyond those half-dozen facts we do not need back-reference to *3 Henry VI* for any but the finer points—so far as the essential ironies of the plot go.

Far more important than these details is the simple overriding principle derived from the Tudor historians: that England rests under a chronic curse—the curse of faction, civil dissension and fundamental anarchy, resulting from the deposition and murder of the Lord's Anointed (Richard II) and the usurpation of the House of Lancaster. The savageries of the Wars of the Roses follow logically (almost theologically) from that; and Elizabeth's "All-seeing heaven, what a world is this!" says but half. It is a world of absolute and hereditary moral ill, in which *everyone* (till the appearance of Richmond-Tudor in Act v) is tainted with the treacheries, the blood and the barbarities of civil strife, and internally blasted with the curse of a moral anarchy which leaves but three human *genera:* the strong in evil, the feebly wicked and the helplessly guilt-tainted (such as the Princes, Anne—all those despairing, lamenting women, whose choric wailings are a penitentional psalm of guilt and sorrow: England's guilt, the individual's sorrow). The "poor painted Queen's" "What a world" needs supplementing with the words of the pessimistically clear-sighted Third Citizen:

> All may be well; but, if God sort it so,
> 'Tis more than we deserve or I expect.
>
> [II. iii. 36]

I have in effect described the meaning of the framework of the play: presented it as "moral history," to be interpreted in abstract terms. But the play itself is also a symphonic structure which I can only describe in terms of music: a rhetorical symphony of five movements, with first and second subjects and some Wagnerian *Leitmotifs.* The play-making framework is Senecan revenge, the characterization largely Marlovian; but the orchestration is not only original, but unique. It can be sketched like this.

The first movement employs five "subjects": Richard himself, his own overture; the wooing-theme (to be repeated in the fourth movement); Richard among his enemies (repeating the duplicity with which he has fooled Clarence); Margaret's curse; and the long dying fall of Clarence. It occupies the whole of Act I.

The second movement includes Act II. and scenes i.-iv. of Act III. It begins with the King's feeble peace-making—in which Buckingham invites his curse—and its other subjects are: a lamentation after the King's death (repeated in the fourth movement); the fall of the curse on Rivers, Grey and Vaughan (when the curse is remembered), and on Hastings (the curse briefly recalled again). The future subject of Richard's moves against the Princes is introduced between-whiles.

The third movement cuts across the Act-divisions and runs from III. v. to IV. iii. Its main subject is the Gloucester-Buckingham plot for the crown, with the magnificently sardonic fooling of the London *bourgeoisie* with a crisis-scare, a brace of bishops, and the headline-story that here is a highly respectable unlibidinous monarch for decent England. On its success, Anne is called to be Queen, and thus to meet the curse she herself called on Richard's wife before he wooed her in that humour and won her (the first movement is here caught up). Buckingham now makes himself one of Richard's future victims by showing reluctance for the plot against the Princes, and Richard throws him off with a snub. The Princes are dealt with (the account of Forrest and Deighton echoing that of the murderers of Clarence, one of whom had a temporary conscience); and Richard concludes with a brisk summary and prospectus:

> The sons of Edward sleep in Abraham's bosom,
> And Anne my wife hath bid this world good night;

and so, since Richmond plans to marry "young Elizabeth, my brother's daughter," "To her go I, a jolly thriving wooer" (Richard's last jocularity). The movement ends with the first murmurs of Richmond. Previously there has been slipped in the trivial-sounding prophecy about "Rugemount," besides Henry VI's prophecy (IV. ii. 99 f.). The flight of the Bishop of Ely (Morton) really troubles Richard.

The fourth movement brings down the curse on Buckingham (v. i. is obviously misplaced, so the movement runs from IV. iv. to v. i. inclusive). Mainly it repeats themes heard before: with a long lamentation-scene (the Blake-like weeping Queens); a repetition of Margaret's curse with the curse of Richard's mother added; the second wooing-scene; the subject of Nemesis repeated by Buckingham. In it the sound of Richmond's advance has become clearer; and Richard's self-command and certainty begin to waver.

The fifth movement is all at Bosworth: the fall of the curse on Richard himself. There is the dream-prologue of the procession of contrapuntal Ghosts (including all those so qualified from the four previous movements) and, like all ghosts, they are reminiscent and repetitive. The play ends with the epilogue to the Wars of the Roses—spoken by Queen Elizabeth's grandfather—calling a blessing on the English future, and inverting the opening lines of Richard's prologue:

> Now is the winter of our discontent
> Made glorious summer . . .

The deliberateness of this highly controlled workmanship needs but little comment. I shall take up a single musical phrase: one that intertwines its plangent undertones throughout the whole symphony, a true *Leitmotif*.

At first sight, Clarence's dream (I. iv. 9 f.) appears to contribute little to the play, nothing to the plot; and it may seem a rhetorical indulgence, even if we accept Mr. Eliot's judgement that it shows "a real approximation in English to the magnificence of Senecan Latin at its best. . . . The

best of Seneca has here been absorbed into English." [1] But first recollect
the setting. Clarence has been sent to the Tower, by the machinations of
the Queen's party (so he thinks), and he is confident that his brother
Richard will stand good friend to him. He believes Richard's worried
"We are not safe, Clarence; we are not safe"; cannot possibly see the
ironical joke Richard is cracking with himself; has no idea that he has
been first on Richard's list since that moment in *3 Henry VI* (v. vi. 84)
when his brother muttered, "Clarence, beware; thou keep'st me from the
light." [2] (A line that follows a passage predetermining the gulling of both
Clarence and Anne to follow:

> I have no brother, I am like no brother;
> And this word "love," which greybeards call divine,
> Be resident in men like one another,
> And not in me! I am myself alone).

Clarence had not been there to hear that: knows nothing of the typically
sharp reversal of Richard's solemnly hypocritical fooling now with:

> Go tread the path that thou shalt ne'er return.
> Simple, plain Clarence, I do love thee so
> That I will shortly send thy soul to heaven,
> If heaven will take the present at our hands.
>
> [ı. i. 117-20]

Clarence has his nightmare in the Tower: a vision prophetic of doom,
and thick with curdled guilt. He dreams that Richard blunderingly knocks
him overboard from a vessel; he drowns; goes to hell; and his guilt-sick
mind spews up its own evil:

> *Keeper:*   Awak'd you not in this sore agony?
> *Clarence:*   No, no, my dream was lengthen'd after life.
>   O, then began the tempest to my soul!
>   I pass'd, methought, the melancholy flood
>   With that sour ferryman which poets write of,
>   Unto the kingdom of perpetual night.

---

[1] *Selected Essays*, 1932, p. 90; reprinted from Introduction to *Seneca His Tenne Tragedies*, 1927.

[2] This contradicts R. G. Moulton, *Shakespeare as a Dramatic Artist*, 1885 (p. 92), who says Richard is *not* "ambitious" (as Macbeth is): "never found dwelling upon the prize in view." This presumes a complete disconnection between *3 Henry VI* and *Richard III*. No such assumption is acceptable nowadays—nor was it sensible even then.

> The first that there did greet my stranger soul
> Was my great father-in-law, renowned Warwick,
> Who spake aloud "What scourge for perjury
> Can this dark monarchy afford false Clarence?"
> And so he vanish'd. Then came wand'ring by
> A shadow like an angel, with bright hair
> Dabbled in blood, and he shriek'd out aloud
> "Clarence is come—false, fleeting, perjur'd Clarence,
> That stabb'd me in the field by Tewkesbury.
> Seize on him, Furies, take him unto torment!"
>
> [I. iv. 42-57]

It is as fine a passage in that style as English can offer: calculated to leave its solemn music in even half-attentive ears. In the second movement of the play (II. ii. 43 f.), Queen Elizabeth announces the King's death:

> If you will live, lament; if die, be brief,
> That our swift-winged souls may catch the King's,
> Or like obedient subjects follow him
> To his new kingdom of ne'er-changing night.

It is scarcely a proper-wifely expectation of the fate of her husband's spirit: but the echo of "Unto the kingdom of perpetual night" is the effect intended, not Elizabeth's notions. The actors who put together the Q. text of 1597 showed that they appreciated, if clumsily, the author's intention. They made it "To his new kingdom of perpetuall rest": catching the echo rightly, while missing the point.

The same "dark monarchy" awaits all these people: they are the living damned. That is the translation of this echo-technique of *Leitmotifs;* and why I call the play's anatomy "musical." Nor is that all: the phrase returns again. But before I come to that, remark how Hastings philosophizes on his fall at the end of the second movement:

> O momentary grace of mortal men,
> Which we more hunt for than the grace of God!
> Who builds his hope in air of your good [3] looks
> Lives like a drunken sailor on a mast,
> Ready with every nod to tumble down
> Into the fatal bowels of the deep.
>
> [III. iv. 98-103]

---

[3] Qq. faire.

We have heard that surging rhythm before. And with it the feeling of being aloft, in air, unbalanced: the rhythm of Clarence dreaming:

> As we pac'd along
> Upon the giddy footing of the hatches,
> Methought that Gloucester stumbled, and in falling
> Struck me, that thought to stay him, overboard
> Into the tumbling billows of the main.
>
> [I. iv. 16-20]

Pattern repeats pattern with remarkable exactitude. "Into the fatal bowels of the deep" is where the giddy Hastings also goes. "O Lord, methought what pain it was to drown" might be extended to all these desperate swimmers in the tide of pomp and history. The elaboration of the dream is no mere exercise in fine phrase on Latin models: it offers a symbol of choking suspense above black depths (the ocean, and perpetual night) which epitomizes the "momentary grace" of all these "mortal men" and women. And the sea as figure of "the destructive element" appears again in Elizabeth's lines in the second wooing-scene:

> But that still use of grief makes wild grief tame,
> My tongue should to thy ears not name my boys
> Till that my nails were anchor'd in thine eyes;
> And I, in such a desp'rate bay of death,
> Like a poor bark, of sails and tackling reft,
> Rush all to pieces on thy rocky bosom.
>
> [IV. iv. 229-34]

"Bay" of death suggests also an animal at bay; just plausibly relevant, since Richard (the boar) would be at bay when she *could* scratch his eyes out. But the repetition of the rather too emphatic anchors and the eyes from Clarence's dream is much more striking.

You will find a further echo of the "night-motif" in the last movement. Richard suspects Stanley (confusingly also called Derby), and reasonably so: for he was husband to the Countess of Richmond, Henry Tudor's mother, the famous Lady Margaret Beaufort; and therefore keeps his son, George Stanley, as hostage. Before Bosworth, he sends a brisk message to warn the father of the black depths beneath the son; and again Shakespeare sounds his doom-music from the Clarence sequence:

> bid him bring his power
> Before sunrising, lest his son George fall
> Into the blind cave of eternal night.
>
> [v. iii. 60-2]

Need I remark that Clarence was "George" too, and lightly called that by Richard when he was afraid that King Edward might die before he signed his brother's death-warrant?

> He cannot live, I hope, and must not die
> Till George be packed with post-horse up to heaven.
>
> [I. ii. 145]

    I could further exemplify the play's tight-woven artistry by taking up that very remarkable prose-speech on "conscience" by Clarence's Second Murderer (I. iv. 133 f.), and following the word into Richard's troubled mind in Act v. before Margaret's curse attains its last fulfilment. But to reduce attention to Richard himself in his own play, beyond what I am already committed to by my insistence on taking the play as a *whole* (as a dramatic pattern, not an exposition of "character"), would be to do it—and Shakespeare—an injustice.

    Richard Plantagenet is alone with Macbeth as the Shakespearian version of the thoroughly bad man in the role of monarch and hero; he is unique in combining with that role that of the diabolic humorist. It is this quality which makes it an inadequate account to say that the play is "moral history," or that the protagonists are the personality of Richard and the curse of Margaret (or what it stood for in orthodox Tudor thinking about retributive justice in history)—for all that these opposed "forces" *are* central throughout. The first movement establishes both, and emphatically. First, Richard, stumping down the stage on his unequal legs, forcing his hitched-up left shoulder and his withered arm on us, till we realize that *this* is what the "winter of our discontent" in *3 Henry VI* has produced, *this* the proper "hatch and brood of time"; and then, Richard established, his cruel and sardonic effectiveness demonstrated on Clarence and Anne, there arises against his brazen Carl Orfflike music the one voice he quails before (if but slightly) the subdominant notes of Margaret and her prophecy of doom, to which the ghosts will walk in the visionary night before Bosworth. It is a conflict between a spirit and a ghost: between Richard, the spirit of ruthless will, of daemonic pride, energy and self-sufficiency, of devilish gusto and *Schadenfreude* (he *enjoys* wickedness even when it is of no practical advantage to his ambitions or to securing himself by murder: it may be only wickedness in *words,* but the spirit revealed is no less evilly exultant for that); and the ghost, as I call her—for what else is Margaret, Reignier's daughter picked up on a battlefield by Suffolk and married to that most etiolated of Shakespeare's husbands, Henry VI, but the living ghost of Lancaster, the walking dead, memorializing the long, cruel, treacherous, bloody conflict of the years of civil strife and pitiless butchery?

You can, of course, see more there if you will. Make her the last stage or age of woman-in-politics: she who has been beautiful, fiercely passionate, queenly, dominating, master of armies, *generalissima;* now old, defeated, empty of everything but fierce bitterness, the illimitable bitterness and rancour of political zeal. What did Yeats write of *his* equivalent symbol? It is in *A Prayer for my Daughter.* For her he prays:

> An intellectual hatred is the worst,
> So let her think opinions are accursed.
> Have I not seen the loveliest woman born
> Out of the mouth of Plenty's horn,
> Because of her opinionated mind
> Barter that horn and every good
> By quiet natures understood
> For an old bellows full of angry wind?

Margaret is that, if you like; but, not to go beyond Shakespeare, I cannot but think that when the old Duchess of York sits down upon the ground for the second lamentation-scene (to tell "sad stories of the death of kings"), the *author's* mind ran more upon Margaret as he wrote:

> Dead life, blind sight, poor mortal living ghost, . . .
> Brief abstract and record of tedious days,
> Rest thy unrest on England's awful earth,
> Unlawfully made drunk with innocent blood.
>
> [IV. iv. 26, 28-30]

Here Shakespeare devises a new variation on the Senecan visitant from another world howling for revenge, by making the spectre nominal flesh and blood; the tune of the Dance of Death to which all dance to damnation is played by Margaret: and one aspect of the play is our watching the rats go into the Weser, compelled by that fatal tune.

But Richard himself is not simply the last and most important (and worst) of the victims—if those justly destroyed can be called "victims." That is just where the label "moral history" is inadequate. For Richard has grown a new dimension since his abrupt and remarkable develop-

ment in *3 Henry VI*: he has become a wit, a mocking comedian, a "vice
of kings"—but with a clear inheritance from the old Vice of the Moralities: part symbol of evil, part comic devil, and chiefly, on the stage, the
generator of roars of laughter at wickednesses (whether of deed or word)
which the audience would immediately condemn in real life. On the one
hand, his literary relations with the Senecan "Tyrant" (author of "In
regna mea Mors impetratur," etc.) are clear enough; as they are with the
Elizabethan myth of "the murderous Machiavel" ("feared am I more than
loved/Let me be feared," etc.): enough has been written on them. But
only the medieval heritage—from the comic devils with their *Schaden-
freude,* and the Vice as comic inverter of order and decency—can fully
explain the new Richard of this apparent sequel to the *Henry VI* series.

I have said that the Christian pattern imposed on history gives the
simple plot of a cast accursed, where all are evil beings, all deserve
punishment. Look, then, with a believing Tudor eye, and ought you not
to *approve* Richard's doings? *Per se,* they are the judgment of God on
the wicked; and he

> *Ein Teil von jener Kraft*
> *Die stets das Böse will, und stets das Gute schafft.*[4]

But that is not all. Richard's sense of humour, his function as clown, his
comic irreverences and sarcastic or sardonic appropriations of things to
(at any rate) *his* occasions: all those act as underminers of our assumed
naïve and proper Tudor principles; and we are on his side much rather
because he makes us (as the Second Murderer put it) "take the devil in
[our] mind," than for any "historical-philosophical-Christian-retribu-
tional" sort of motive. In this respect a good third of the play is a kind
of grisly *comedy;* in which we meet the fools to be taken in on Richard's
terms, see them with his mind, and rejoice with him in their stultification
(in which execution is the ultimate and unanswerable practical joke, the
absolutely final laugh this side of the Day of Judgment). Here, Richard
is a middle-term between Barabas, the Jew of Malta (*c.* 1590) and Vol-
pone (1606). He inhabits a world where everyone deserves everything he
can do to them; and in his murderous practical joking he is *inclusively*
the comic exposer of the mental shortcomings (the intellectual and moral
deformities) of this world of beings depraved and besotted. If we forget to
pity them awhile (and he does his best to help us), then his impish spirit
urges us towards a positive reversal of "Christian charity" until the play's

---

[4] "A part of that Power which always wills evil and yet always brings about good."
(Goethe's *Faust*)

fourth movement (which is when the Elizabethan spectator began to back out, I take it)—or even beyond that point.

An aspect of Richard's appeal, which has, I fancy, passed relatively unexamined,[5] is one that we can be confident that William Shakespeare felt and reflected on. I mean the appeal of the actor: the talented being who can assume every mood and passion at will, at all events to the extent of making others believe in it. Beyond question, all our great actors have regarded the part as a fine opportunity. The extent to which the histrionic art (as Shakespeare thought and felt about it) contributed to the making of this great stage-figure is to me more interesting.

The specific interest here is the *power* that would be in the hands of an actor consummate enough to make (quite literally) "all the world a stage" and to work on humanity by the perfect simulation of every feeling: the appropriate delivery of every word and phrase that will serve his immediate purpose; together with the complete dissimulation of everything that might betray him (whether it be his intentions, or such obstructive feelings as compunction, pity or uncertainty of mind). This appears at once when Gloucester first takes shape as the man self-made to be King, in the long soliloquy in *3 Henry VI* (III. ii. 124 f.). The closing lines are specifically on histrionic genius:

> Why, I can smile, and murder whiles I smile,
> And cry "Content!" to that which grieves my heart,
> And wet my cheeks with artificial tears,
> And frame my face to all occasions.
>
> [ibid. 182-5]

And then, after a little bragging prospectus on his intended deadliness, he ends:

> I can add colours to the chameleon,
> Change shapes with Proteus for advantages,
> And set the murderous Machiavel to school.
> Can I do this, and cannot get a crown?
> Tut, were it farther off, I'll pluck it down.
>
> [ibid. 191-5]

M. R. Ridley notes here that "Machiavelli . . . seems to have been to the Elizabethans a type of one who advocated murder as a method of

---

[5] [J. Middleton Murry, *Shakespeare*, 1936, pp. 125-6, quotes the theatrical metaphors and remarks briefly on the conception of Richard as an actor.] (*Ed. note*)

cold-blooded policy." [6] It is true that that marks off one point of difference between the "Senecan" tyrant-villainy (which is primarily for revenge) and the "Machiavellian" (which is for power, or self-aggrandizement: "We that are great, our own self-good still moves us"): though I do not think that the distinction can be maintained, if you read Seneca. But surely Ridley's note misses the point, in its context? What the "Machiavel" allusion represents is, I believe, Shakespeare's recognition that the programme set before the Prince in *Il Principe* is one that demands exactly those histrionic qualities I have just described: a lifelong, unremitting vigilance in relentless simulation and impenetrable deception. There, precisely, lies the super-humanity of the Superman. The will-to-power is shorn of its effective power without it. He is an *artist* in evil.

Now Richard in his own play shows this power—these powers—to perfection. Except to the audience, he is invisible; but the audience he keeps reminded not only of his real intentions, but equally of his actor's artistries. The bluff plain Englishman, shocked at ambitious go-getters and grievingly misunderstood, is perfectly "done" before the Queen's relations:

> Because I cannot flatter and look fair,
> Smile in men's faces, smooth, deceive, and cog,
> Duck with French nods and apish courtesy,
> I must be held a rancorous enemy.
> Cannot a plain man live and think no harm
> But thus his simple truth must be abus'd
> With silken, sly, insinuating Jacks?
>
> [I. iii. 47-53]

A little later, it is: "I am too childish-foolish for this world," (ibid., 142); and even: "I thank my God for my humility." (II. i. 72).

Then, left to himself and the audience, after egging on all their quarrels:

> But then I sigh and, with a piece of Scripture,
> Tell them that God bids us do good for evil.
> And thus I clothe my naked villainy
> With odd old ends stol'n forth of holy writ,
> And seem a saint when most I play the devil.
>
> [I. iii. 334-8]

---

[6] *New Temple* edn., p. 140.

The stage-direction, *"Enter two Murderers,"* caps this nicely. It is not simply that Richard is a hypocrite and (like other stage villains) tells us so. The actor's technique of "asides" is the essence of his chuckling private jokes—made to "myself alone." (You might say that Shakespeare is giving not merely "the acting of drama," but also "the drama of consummate *acting*").

The same reminders, nudging the audience's attention, appear in his swift-switched actual asides: e.g., his thoroughly unholy reception of his mother's blessing, spoken as he gets up off his dutiful knees:

> Amen! And make me die a good old man!
> That is the butt end of a mother's blessing;
> I marvel that her Grace did leave it out.
>
> [II. ii. 109-11]

Or, again, we have Richard's insinuating equivocations in talking to the prattling little Princes; in one of which he acknowledges his theatrical-historical legacy from the Moralities: "Thus, like the formal vice, Iniquity,/I moralize two meanings in one word." (III. i. 82-3). Over and above this there is that striking passage (III. v. 1-11) where he and Buckingham are working up a crisis (appearing ill-dressed in old rusty armour, as if they had armed in desperate haste), when Richard specifically inquires whether Buckingham can "do the stage-tragedian":

> *Richard:*   Come, cousin, canst thou quake and change thy colour,
>   Murder thy breath in middle of a word,
>   And then again begin, and stop again,
>   As if thou wert distraught and mad with terror?
> *Buckingham:* Tut, I can counterfeit the deep tragedian;
>   Speak and look back, and pry on every side,
>   Tremble and start at wagging of a straw,
>   Intending deep suspicion. Ghastly looks
>   Are at my service, like enforced smiles;
>   And both are ready in their offices
>   At any time to grace my stratagems.

It is all sardonically jocular; but nothing shows more clearly the artist's delight in his craft: call it illusion or deception, it makes no odds. It is this dexterity that his other rapid reversals of tone keep us aware of; whether he is half-amazedly rejoicing in his conquest of Anne, or poking unfilial fun at his mother (a performance more shocking to Elizabethans than to our more child-foolish days).

Yet again, there is that admirable moment when the Londoners are being fooled into believing that he must be persuaded to be king; when Buckingham pretends to lose patience, with "Zounds, I'll entreat no more." And Richard, bracketed aloft with two Bishops, is distressed: "O, do not swear, my lord of Buckingham." (III. vii. 220). (It is like the moment in *Eric or Little by Little* (ch. 8) when Eric refers to the usher as a "surly devil"; and the virtuous Russell exclaims: "O Eric, that is the first time that I have heard you swear.") It is this unholy jocularity, the readiness of sarcastic, sardonic, profane and sometimes blasphemous wit, the demonic gusto of it all, which not only wins the audience over to accepting the Devil as hero, but also points us towards the central paradox of the play. And, through that, to a full critical awareness of its unity: with a few remarks on which I shall conclude.

To begin with Richard. On the face of it, he is the demon-Prince, the cacodemon born of hell, the misshapen toad, etc. (all things ugly and ill). But through his prowess as actor and his embodiment of the comic Vice and impish-to-fiendish humour, he offers the false as more attractive than the true (the actor's function), and the ugly and evil as admirable and amusing (the clown's game of value-reversals). You can say, "We don't take him seriously." I reply, "That is exactly what gets most of his acquaintances into Hell: just what the devil-clown relies on." But he is not only this demon incarnate, he is in effect God's agent in a predetermined plan of divine retribution: the "scourge of God." Now by Tudor-Christian historical principles, this plan is *right*. Thus, in a real sense, Richard is a King who "can do no wrong"; for in the pattern of the justice of divine retribution on the wicked, he functions as an avenging angel. Hence my paradoxical title, "Angel with Horns."

The paradox is sharpened by what I have mainly passed by: the repulsiveness, humanely speaking, of the "justice." God's will it may be, but it sickens us: it is as pitiless as the Devil's (who is called in to execute it). The contrast with Marlowe's painless, dehumanized slaughterings in *Tamburlaine* is patent.

This overall system of *paradox* is the play's unity. It is revealed as a constant displaying of inversions, or reversals of meaning: whether we consider the verbal patterns (the *peripeteias* or reversals of act and intention or expectation); the antithesis of false and true in the histrionic character; or the constant inversions of irony. Those verbal capsizings I began by talking about, with their deliberate reversals to the opposite meaning in equivocal terms, are the exact correlatives of both the nature of man (or man in power: Richard) and of the nature of events (history); and of language too, in which all is conveyed.

But, start where you will, you come back to history; or to the pattern made out of the conflict of two "historical myths." The orthodox Tudor myth made history God-controlled, divinely prescribed and dispensed, to move things towards a God-ordained perfection: Tudor England. Such was the *frame* that Shakespeare took. But the total effect of Shakespeare's "plot" has quite a different effect from Halle: a very different meaning. Dr. Duthie may write, "But there is no doubt that Shakespeare saw history in the same light as Halle saw it." [7] I say there *is* doubt. Dover Wilson has nothing to offer but what he summarizes from Moulton, but his last sentence points my doubting way: "it appears, to me at least, unlikely that Shakespeare's 'main end' in *Richard III* was 'to show the working out of God's will in English history.' "[8] (The quotation he is discussing is from Tillyard's *Shakespeare's History Plays* (1944), p. 208.) He can go no further because his own limitations on *Henry IV* inhibit his ever observing that the comic Richard has no more place in Halle's scheme than Falstaff has.

The other myth is that of Richard the Devil-King: the Crookback *monstrum deforme, ingens* whom Shakespeare *found* as a ready-made Senecan tyrant and converted into a quite different inverter of moral order: a ruthless, demonic comedian with a most un-Senecan sense of humour and the seductive appeal of an irresistible gusto, besides his volcanic Renaissance energies. They are themselves demoralizing: *Tapfer sein ist gut*[9] is the antithesis of a Christian sentiment.

The outcome of this conflict of myths was Shakespeare's display of constant inversions of meaning; in all of which, two systems of meaning impinge and go over to their opposites, like the two "ways" of the cheveril glove. This applies equally to words and word-patterns; to the actor-nature; to dramatic ironies; and to events, as the hatch and brood of time, contrasted with opposite expectations.

As a result of the paradoxical ironic structure built from these inversions of meaning—built above all by Richard's demonic appeal—the naïve, optimistic, "Christian" principle of history, consoling and comfortable, modulates into its opposite. The "Christian" system of retribution is undermined, counterbalanced, by historic irony. (Do I need to insist that the coupling of "Christian" and "retribution" itself is a paradox? That the God of vengeance is *not* a Christian God; that his opposite is a God of mercy who has no representation in this play. If I do, I had

---

[7] G. I. Duthie, *Shakespeare*, 1951, p. 118.
[8] *Richard III* (*New Cambridge* edn., 1954), p. xlv.
[9] "To be bold is good."

better add that the so-called "Christian" frame is indistinguishable from a pagan one of Nemesis in which the "High all-seer" is a Fate with a cruel sense of humour.)

But do not suppose I am saying that the play is a "debunking of Tudor myth," or that Shakespeare is disproving it. He is not "proving" anything: not even that "Blind belief is sure to err/And scan his works in vain" (though I think that is *shown*, nevertheless). Contemporary "order"-thought spoke as if naïve faith saw true: God was above God's Englishmen and ruled with justice—which meant summary vengeance. This historic myth offered absolutes, certainties. Shakespeare in the Histories always leaves us with relatives, ambiguities, irony, a process thoroughly dialectical. Had he entirely accepted the Tudor myth, the frame and pattern of order, his way would have led, I suppose, towards writing *moral history* (which is what Dr. Tillyard and Dr. Dover Wilson and Professor Duthie have made *out* of him). Instead, his way led him towards writing *comic history*. The former would never have taken him to tragedy: the latter (paradoxically) did. Look the right way through the cruel-comic side of Richard and you glimpse Iago. Look back at him through his energy presented as evil, and you see Macbeth. And if you look at the irony of men's struggles in the nets of historic circumstance, the ironies of their pride and self-assurance, you will see Coriolanus; and you are past the great tragic phase and back in history again.

Commodity and Honour
in *King John*

by James L. Calderwood

Most critics of *King John*, even since the advent of the now no longer
new criticism, have given their attention chiefly to the source problems of
the play, especially to the relationship between *King John* and *The
Troublesome Raigne*. As one result Shakespeare's play as a work of art
in its own right has largely been ignored. The sporadic vigour of its verse
and the vitality of the Bastard have often been remarked—the Bastard's
Commodity speech is usually cited as a conspicuous example of both—
but not so much for what they accomplish in the play as for what they
tell us about Shakespeare's maturing dramatic powers, that is, for what
light they cast before and after, but not on, the play in which they appear. Although the Commodity speech is indeed central to *King John*, it
serves as more than an isolated instance of Shakespeare's progress from
ceremonious rhetoric to a more lean and trenchant utterance: it not
only underscores the principle of Commodity as one of the prevailing
forces in men's lives, but by the extremity of its statement it also suggests
the ethical imbalance which runs through the play. The view I am
proposing is that *King John* represents a dramatic crucible in which
Shakespeare explores and tests two antagonistic ethical principles, Commodity and Honour. The opposition between Commodity, or scheming
self-interest, and Honour, loyalty in general but in its highest form
loyalty to the good of England, comprises a basic theme to which almost
every action and character of the play is vitally related. In its political
implications the theme explores the qualities demanded of the kingly
character; in its general pervasiveness and in its specific application to

"Commodity and Honour in *King John*," by James L. Calderwood. From the *University of Toronto Quarterly*, XXIX (1960), 341-56. Copyright © 1960 by the University
of Toronto Press. Reprinted by permission of the author and the University of Toronto
Press.

John and the Bastard, it imparts to the play a unity of structure generally denied it.[1]

Both elements of this theme are conspicuous early in Act I when the Bastard is offered a choice between personal gain—the land now declared legally his—and the honour of being acknowledged Cœur-de-lion's son. In accepting the latter, however, the Bastard does not choose nobly to sacrifice self-interest. Honour only apparently has much to do with his decision; he clearly associates it with Cœur-de-lion when he tells John that his supposed father, Faulconbridge, was "A soldier by the honour-giving hand/Of Cœur-de-lion knighted in the field." [2] But later, speaking to his now half-brother, he oversimplifies the alternatives when he says, "My father gave me honour, yours gave land." At the moment of choice he did not actually believe himself the son of Cœur-de-lion—later in the scene he solicits his mother for his real father's name. Instead, he had accepted honour as an investment in the future—"Brother, take you my land, I'll take my chance"—gambling on the "chance" that his continued association with John and Eleanor would produce dividends. His choice, then, has involved a public proclamation of honour, a private acceptance of self-interest. As we shall see later, this is the principal strategy by which Commodity makes its "smooth-faced" way in the world of *King John*. But, as we shall also see, the Bastard's motives in this scene undergo a change, or, more precisely, they pass through a series of changes that constitutes one of the first explorations which this play makes of the relationship between Commodity and Honour.

When he makes his choice, and immediately afterwards, the Bastard embraces self-interest while professing honour; but once he has achieved his immediate aim, the mocking and even flippant ironies of his speech assume a different cast. The opening lines of his first soliloquy are suggestive:

> Brother, adieu; good fortune come to thee!
> For thou wast got i' th' way of honesty.
> *(Exeunt all but Bastard.)*
> A foot of honour better than I was;
> But many a foot of land the worse.

---

[1] Adrien Bonjour, in "The Road to Swinstead Abbey," *ELH*, XVIII (1951), offers the best, and indeed almost the only, defense of the structure of *King John*. All further references to Bonjour are to this article.

[2] The text I am using is that of Neilson and Hill in *The Complete Plays and Poems of William Shakespeare* (Cambridge, 1942).

The public graciousness is subjected, after the exit, to the diminution of private irony, the "way of honesty" to the measure of material gain. But the admission is also made, and privately, that the gain of new honour has been attended by the loss of old honour—legitimacy. The ambiguity of statement mirrors while it explores the ambivalence of the Bastard's moral self-consciousness. Yet it is only after he learns the truth of his parentage that he becomes genuinely involved with his new identity and graduates from the endorsement of honour as a pragmatic good to an avowal of it even against social scorn. The violence of his advocacy of his mother here is not, despite surface resemblances, the brash impetuosity of a Hotspur; it follows logically from, and reflexively illuminates, the fact that his soliloquy on "new-made honour" was self-satire as well as social satire. However, if in this first scene we are seeing the Bastard's growth of moral awareness, that growth is still embryonic. At the conclusion of the scene his conception of honour, though altered, remains unsophisticated; it is regarded less as the inherence of ethical values than as a transferable award which one can receive through inheritance or merit through physical exploit. The Bastard has not yet outgrown Hotspur. Nevertheless he has formed one resolution which we would do well to remember. Observing that flattery and deceit serve as "sweet poison for the age's tooth," he adds, "Which, though I will not practise to deceive/Yet, to avoid deceit, I mean to learn."

In Act II, lines 156-8, another choice is offered, not to the Bastard but to Arthur. The alternatives, however, are not the same as earlier. When John says,

> Arthur of Bretagne, yield thee to my hand,
> And out of my dear love I'll give thee more
> Than e'er the coward hand of France can win . . .

he not only characterizes the motives of France, and of himself, but also places Arthur in the position of having to choose between two kinds of Commodity and thus to announce by implication his self-interestedness. Arthur remains silent, refusing the terms of the choice not because he recognizes the phrasings of deceit but simply because he is utterly lacking in self-interest—"I am not worth this coil that's made for me." Constance, however, has no scruples about choosing for him, and she is willing to take what the "hand of France can win." Her self-interest is masked, not consciously perhaps, within the *cliché* of doting motherhood, and Eleanor is probably close to the truth when she says, "Out,

insolent! thy bastard shall be king/That thou mayst be a queen, and
check the world!"—which, incidentally, tells us as much about accuser as
about accused. What Constance fails to realize, however, is the pervasiveness of Commodity. Perceiving it in John, she does not see that it is
also the "bias of the world." It is perhaps because her own self-interest is
not consciously masked that she fails to penetrate the conscious masks of
others—of France in particular. Certainly a clearer awareness of the issues
involved would have made her realize the irrelevance of exhorting
Lewis to defy John on the basis of "thine honour, Lewis, thine honour!"

The position of Constance and Arthur is analogous to that of Blanche,
who, like Arthur, achieves a genuine alliance with Honour only to find
that Commodity, that "daily break-vow, he that wins of all," wins most
from those who are innocently unaware of his nature. Only Blanche and
the Bastard are untainted by the epidemic of deceit in which the marriage of expediency is conceived. Spurred by Eleanor to "Urge them while
their souls/Are capable of this ambition," John delivers his proposal to
France (Act II, scene 1, lines 484-6):

> If that the Dauphin there, thy princely son,
> Can in this book of beauty read, "I love,"
> Her dowry shall weigh equal with a queen.

France hastily directs Lewis' attention to Blanche's face, and in that
"book of beauty" Lewis finds, with remarkable decision, that he can
indeed read *I love*. In fact, he reads it aloud and so grandiloquently that
he draws the Bastard's immediate scorn for such patent dissemblance.
Blanche informs Lewis in private that she is subservient to John's royal
will; however, refusing to participate in the general deceit, she candidly
adds, "Further I will not flatter you, my lord,/That all I see in you is
worthy love." Despite her private misgivings, when John asks for her
decision Blanche publicly pledges him her loyalty by saying, "That she
is bound in honour still to do/What you in wisdom still vouchsafe to
say." But in the world of *King John* this sort of honour, so innocent as to
misconstrue Commodity as "wisdom," has little survival value. After her
marriage and with the renewal of war, Blanche strives to expand her
honour to encompass her obligations to both John and her husband
Lewis. The result, as she says (Act III, scene 1, lines 328-30), is that

> I am with both; each army hath a hand,
> And in their rage, I having hold of both,
> They whirl assunder and dismember me.

Like Arthur, Blanche represents honour in a world of Commodity, and like Arthur, she is whirled by the forces of Commodity to her destruction. Despite its dominant station in the hierarchy of men's motives, Commodity by no means receives the stamp of Shakespeare's dramatic approval. If it is the force against which Honour is tested, it is itself in turn tested by Honour. Whirled asunder by the two armies of Commodity, Blanche is not an object of derision but of sympathy. Yet the Honour she has embraced is found wanting—deficient because it is naïve, because it is untempered by awareness, because it has survived no inner tests. Untested within, it succumbs inevitably to the test of Commodity from without. Blanche, like York in *Richard II,* yields to the will of her sovereign in the best accord with Tudor Doctrine; but her problem, like York's, is complicated by the presence of two sovereigns. If Shakespeare is glancing at Tudor Doctrine, then, as Lily Campbell feels he so often is,[3] it is not to extol that doctrine so much as to explore it, to test it dramatically, not in political but in human terms. The judgment of the drama is that the doctrine is simply too inflexible, too arbitrary, too unrealistic. Blanche's attempt to solve her insoluble dilemma leads to her destruction; York, reading the script of Tudor Doctrine with strict literalness, acts out his proper rôle and in doing so is deprived of essential humanity. Nevertheless, Shakespeare is no more deluded by the efficacy of Commodity than he is by the virtue of Honour; in the very process of discrediting Honour, Commodity is itself discredited. That is, if there is any suspicion that Shakespeare is endorsing Commodity in *King John,* it should be dispelled by observing that Commodity is the means by which Shakespeare achieves satiric diminution in the play. Austria, France, and Lewis, not to mention John, are all rendered ridiculous by the very fact that even among men so thoroughly Commodity-conscious, Commodity must be concealed behind a façade of Honour. The rents in the façade are the windows of dramatic deflation, as we can see, perhaps more clearly, with the English nobles.

Salisbury and Pembroke have been too often regarded as a momentarily dissonant but then beautifully harmonic chorus singing the praises of national unity for English audiences intensely patriotic following the defeat of the Spanish armada. If this is all that Shakespeare's audiences saw in the nobles—and there is no guarantee of that—then Shakespeare was giving his audiences a good deal more than they deserved. To begin with, the nobles' criticism of John's second coronation (Act IV, scene 2) is not, as it might seem, merely the constructive advice of loyal subjects. We should note the opening of the following scene:

---

[3] *Shakespeare's "Histories": Mirrors of Elizabethan Policy* (San Marino, 1947).

SAL.   Lords, I will meet him at Saint Edmundsbury.
        It is our safety, and we must embrace
        This gentle offer of the perilous time.
PEM.   Who brought that letter from the Cardinal?
SAL.   The Count Melun, a noble lord of France;
        Whose private with me of the Dauphin's love
        Is much more general than these lines import.

The Bastard's greeting a moment later—"Once more to-day well met, distempered lords"—establishes the day of this exchange as still that of the previous scene. Either the nobles have been in communication with the Dauphin for some time then, or Melun's delivery of the letter to Salisbury represents Lewis' first overture. If the former is true, the nobles clearly were traitorous even before their criticism of John in scene 2, and if the latter is true, Lewis must have had some prior indication of their willingness to cooperate, else why send Melun to these particular nobles? In either event, suspicion is cast upon the nobles' high indignation at the announcement of Arthur's supposed death; and their protestations of dutiful subservience to John in the same scene (e.g., Salisbury's "Since all and every part of what we would/Doth make a stand at what your Highness will," Act IV, scene 2) acquire retrospectively an ironic, if not a hypocritical, cast. Moreover, knowing that the nobles have already decided for their "safety" to embrace the "gentle offer of the perilous time," we can see that in their speeches over Arthur's body, Commodity, now motivating treason, has become for Shakespeare a most incisive means for subverting the lofty pretensions of offended Honour. Tillyard has rightly observed that "the levity of [the nobles'] reasoning" here is betrayed "by the extravagance of their sentiments";[4] however, the point is not so much that their reasoning is specious logically as that it is specious ethically. If their premise of Commodity is granted, their real reasoning is sound, if not terribly subtle: to take advantage of an ideally fortuitous opportunity for masking dishonourable action behind honourable indignation. Their rôles are overacted, to be sure—especially Salisbury's, whose 25 lines of bombast are as devoid of genuine sorrow as the Bastard's single sentence is freighted with it. Pembroke, however, displays their real line of reasoning and demonstrates at the same time considerable genius for rationalization when he says that the heinousness of Arthur's murder "Shall give a holiness, a purity,/To the yet unbegotten sin of times"—for example, he would probably add, the not quite unbegotten sin of their own imminent treason.

⁴ *Shakespeare's History Plays* (New York, 1946), 223.

When we see them next (Act V, scene 2), the nobles are still cloaking Commodity in the vestments of Honour. The business of signing to treason dispatched, Salisbury laments for 31 lines, all after the fact, that

> . . . such is the infection of the time,
> That, for the health and physic of our right,
> We cannot deal but with the very hand
> Of stern injustice and confused wrong.

He is perfectly accurate in everything, provided "right" be changed to read "profit"; and his conclusion, with its wish that "these two Christian armies might combine/The blood of malice in a vein of league," would be impressive indeed, if it did not remind us that the two nations already joined once in such a league—the very league that called forth the Bastard's speech on Commodity. Or again, when Salisbury's grief produces what Lewis calls "this honourable dew/That silverly doth progress on thy cheeks," it is a little difficult not to hear an echo of Salisbury's own comment when Hubert wept at the sight of Arthur's body: "Trust not those cunning waters of his eyes,/For villainy is not without such rheum." Although Lewis' answering speech is as fraught with noble sentiment as was Salisbury's, it is quite clear that both are speaking the language of ceremony on a stage of Honour. Even Lewis finally wearies of the extended hypocrisy and puts the matter in its real light by saying,

> Come, come; for thou shalt thrust thy hand as deep
> Into the purse of rich prosperity
> As Lewis himself; so, nobles, shall you all. . . .

Needless to say, this view of Salisbury and Pembroke implies that their final and seemingly glorious reversion to the English cause should be regarded with more than a little suspicion. Before dealing with that, however, let us return to the first half of the play again and examine John and the Bastard in the light of the theme we have been tracing. In the opening act we saw Shakespeare using the Bastard's changing attitudes towards Commodity and Honour as indices of his ethical development. Later, in Blanche, we saw internally untested Honour tested externally by and succumbing to the pressures of Commodity, and still later, in the English nobles, we saw Commodity used as a satiric device to deflate pretensions of Honour. In all these instances Commodity and Honour were Shakespeare's principal means of characterization, and he also uses them to characterize John and the Bastard. We should not forget, however, that the process works reciprocally, that the persons in the drama are not only characterized by, but also characterize, the ethical principles. By her adherence to Honour in a world of Commodity, Blanche is characterized as honourable in what would seem to be an ideally pure manner. Yet she in turn, by proving too innocent to survive the pressures of Commodity, characterizes pure Honour as an impracticable moral guide. The nobles, on the other hand, have survived and even prospered so far largely because their Commodity was not unadulterated, because they were not unaware of at least the habiliments of Honour and of the manner in which these can be worn to further the ends of Commodity. Their successful application of Commodity, however, is such only within the illusion of life created by the drama; their successes within are simultaneously failures from without, from the perspective of audience or reader, and the inversion of effect is produced by satiric techniques. With the nobles we have seen Commodity thrust to the extreme of treason; with John we shall see it thrust to the extreme of murder.

During the first, and inferior, half of the play John represents for the most part "An English King," in Tillyard's phrase. Although his occupation of the throne is for self-interest, yet his interests coincide up to a point with those of England, for despite his virtues Arthur hardly qualifies as a desirable king. His youth, the domination of Constance, and the partisanship of the French all argue against the application of the rule of primogeniture. At any rate, when the play opens John not only is king but is kingly. He also has, significantly, the approval of Fortune.

As in *Richard III,* but less obtrusively, the supernatural invades the field of human action in *King John.* Events are determined by decisions based upon either Commodity or Honour, but once the human decisions have been made, a supernatural judgment is pronounced upon them. Sometimes these judgments take the form of prophecy or of prophetic invocation—as with Constance, Pandulph, and Pomfret; at others they are to be inferred from the behaviour of wind and sea; at still others they are identified as a quality of "the times." For example, early in Act II Fortune graces John's decision to invade France through the instrument of the unfavourable, to France, winds which delay Chatillon's return to warn King Philip. In Act IV, scene 2, when John receives tidings of the French invasion, Fortune has shifted sides. Early in Act III Constance confirms the fact that John still stands in grace when she tells Arthur that Fortune "adulterates hourly with thine uncle John." It is at this point, however, that John's fortunes begin to change for the worse. He and Philip have just negotiated the betrothal of Blanche and Lewis, the bargain that elicited the Bastard's speech on Commodity. The indignant Constance delivers a prophetic invocation that "No bargains break that are not this day made./This day, all things begun come to ill end." (Act III, scene 1, lines 93-4.) The bargain marriage league is indeed immediately broken, and John, who has begun to act upon Commodity, has made the first fatal step on the road to an "ill end."

Since John does win the ensuing battle with France, it would appear that he still remains in grace. But the victory and the capture of Arthur are at best a mixed blessing. Combining the agents of wind and sea in his metaphor, Philip (Act III, scene 4) implies that Fortune is still with John:

> So, by a roaring tempest on the flood,
> A whole armado of convicted sail
> Is scattered and disjoin'd from fellowship.

However, Pandulph immediately assures him that "all shall yet go well," and a little later in this scene Pandulph says to Lewis:

> No, no; when Fortune means to men most good,
> She looks upon them with a threat'ning eye.
> Tis strange to think how much King John hath lost
> In this which he accounts so clearly won.

Thus, although seeming to have remained the same, John's fortunes have actually altered in accordance with Constance's prophecy. But the Commodity marriage is not the sole or the most important reason for the decline of John's fortunes; it is only a prelude to the central scene of *King John* (Act III, scene 3) where the superb dramatic tension created by John's Iago-like probings of Hubert culminates in the terse agreement to murder Arthur:

> K. JOHN.   Death.
> HUB.   My Lord?
> K. JOHN.   A grave.
> HUB.   He shall not live.

This scene is central to *King John* both thematically and structurally. Having condemned to death the one person who utterly lacks a sense of self-interest, John serves both to damn and to be damned by Commodity. Prior to this scene the pace of the play has been leisurely, the action deliberate, the scope of events wide. From this point on the scope narrows and the action becomes precipitous; scene now gives way to scene with abruptness and rapidity as the structure of the play mirrors while it helps display John's hurtle towards destruction. Fortune has clearly shifted, and as Pandulph says to the temporarily dispirited Lewis (Act III, scene 4, lines 146-8):

> John lays you plots; the times conspire with you;
> For he that steeps his safety in true blood
> Shall find but bloody safety and untrue.

In the scene in which Hubert threatens to put out Arthur's eyes (Act IV, scene 1), the current of the action momentarily eddies. The scene has been much maligned for many good reasons, but the blatant sentimentality does serve a dramatic purpose. The principal function of the scene is to intensify John's guilt by a graphic dilation upon the cruelty of his intentions towards Arthur. This intensification of guilt is partly accomplished by contrasting John's orders with Hubert's attempts to carry them out, for if in John Commodity is now motivating cruelty and murder, in Hubert it is being sacrificed to Honour and mercy. Arthur is again the epitome of selflessness. Hubert has accepted John's commission partly from blind loyalty and partly from a desire for gain; however, when he finally relents, Hubert clearly renounces self-interest: "I will not touch thine eye/For all the treasure that thine uncle owes." His decision constitutes not only a renunciation but also an endangering of his self-interest—"Much danger do I undergo for thee." Hubert's later treatment at the hands of John and the English nobles illustrates once more that in *King John* Honour must be its own reward.

During the first half of the play the Bastard—"that mixture of greatness and levity," as Dr. Johnson saw him—is motivated by a spurious sense of Honour alloyed with some amount of self-interest. His levity rather than his greatness predominates. He is brash and reckless, quick both to perceive and to offer insult. His major interest is in acquiring prestige by avenging his father's death at the hands of Austria. However, his resolution in Act I to learn the ways of deceit, not to employ them but to recognize their employment by others, has not gone unobserved. In Act II not only is he a sardonic critic of hypocrisy and pseudo-chivalric bravado but he is also an ironic parodist of the absurd extremes to which Commodity inclines kings and armies. When the Citizen of Angiers (or Hubert, as the First Folio more logically has it) denies both armies entrance to the city, the Bastard with tongue in cheek exhorts

John and Philip to join forces temporarily and, as John paraphrases him a moment later, "lay this Angiers even with the ground;/Then after fight who shall be king of it." Their acceptance of his ironic proposal reveals the folly to which men are led when a myopic preoccupation with schemes of self-interest blinds them to the fact that means may destroy ends. The *reductio ad absurdum* of Commodity has been reached.

However, the Bastard's ethics are by no means unquestionable. If he can recognize and deflate Commodity, yet he is willing to fight in one of its armies. Even his criticism of Commodity prior to the Commodity speech lacks the solidity of moral conviction, and when this criticism culminates in the Commodity speech it is not to renounce but to embrace Commodity. Both Tillyard and Bonjour contend that the final lines of the speech—"Since kings break faith upon Commodity,/Gain, be my lord, for I will worship thee"—are uttered merely in self-deprecation and that the Bastard never acts upon them. I agree that he is incapable of real villainy, and yet the commission John gives him to ransack the monasteries is obviously a reward for his rescue of Eleanor and his acquittal of himself in battle. To be sure, there is no mention of his having profited from the enterprise; however, the very nature of the commission would seem to imply tacitly that some of the liberated "angels" should be reincarcerated in the Bastard's pocket. At any rate, at the conclusion of Act III neither the Bastard nor John represents the lack of self-interest or the sense of responsibility to England demanded of the kingly character.

Act IV, scene 1, as mentioned earlier, serves to intensify John's guilt; and in scene 2 we find that the nobles have grown seditious. John's second coronation is a touchstone of his political insecurity. His situation worsens when Hubert falsely reports Arthur's death. Attempting to see John as a tragic hero, Bonjour finds him genuinely repenting his decision to do away with Arthur. Certainly he regrets the decision once the supposed murder is announced, but it is difficult to believe that his regret is based on anything but the failure of the murder to serve his designs. When the nobles stalk out, John says, "They burn in indignation. I repent," and the juxtaposition of his political loss with his personal repentance is too obvious not to suggest a causal relation. Further on, when Hubert informs him that Arthur is not dead after all, John says, "Doth Arthur live? O, haste thee to the peers," and again the immediacy with which his thoughts flit from Arthur to his own political interests is revealing. Finally, since his desire for Arthur's death was rooted in Commodity, any genuine repentance on his part would involve a renunciation of Commodity. Instead, our next glimpse of him shows him in the act of capitulating to Pandulph (Act V, scene 1), not of course for

religious reasons but merely for Commodity. Receiving the crown back
from Pandulph, he says:

> Now keep your holy word. Go meet the French,
> And from his Holiness use all your power
> To stop their marches 'fore we are inflam'd.

Clearly, the exchange of the crown carries the same stamp as the marriage
league of Act II: it is merely a bargain entered into by John to prevent
his deposition by the French.[5]

If John has sunk to contemptible depths of Commodity, even to the
point of shaming An English King, the Bastard has steadily risen towards
the genuine Honour befitting An English King. His words over the body
of Arthur are the major indication of his spiritual growth; yet without
some preparation this speech would mark an altogether too abrupt deepening of character—and Shakespeare provides the preparation. Returning from his forays upon the monasteries (Act IV, scene 2) the Bastard
meets the irate departing nobles—"With eyes as red as new-enkindled
fire," as he tells John. His first words to John are hardly respectful: "But
if you be afeard to hear the worst,/Then let the worst unheard fall on
your head." Throughout this scene his remarks to John are terse and
restrained, suggesting a grave preoccupation. Disturbed by rumours and
prophecies abroad, by news of the invading French and by the report
of Arthur's death, he cannot help but suspect John. His remark that he
has seen the nobles

> And others more, going to seek the grave
> Of Arthur, whom they say is kill'd to-night
> On your suggestion,

is most carefully phrased. He withholds comment on the nobles' accusa-
tion and in doing so tactfully offers John a chance to deny his guilt. It
is in this scene that we see the Bastard beginning to make a distinction
between An English King and the man John as king. His respect for
the former prevents him from too hastily condemning the latter. Already

---

[5] Further evidence that John's exchange of the crown is rooted in Commodity can
be found in his remark when he sends the Bastard after the nobles: "I have a way
to win their loves again./Bring them before me," (Act IV, scene 2, lines 169-70). Since
John does not yet know that Arthur is alive, this cannot be his "way to win their loves
again." Instead, it seems clear that he has already decided to use Pandulph as a means
of stopping the French. His self-deposition is thus merely a tactic by which to insure
his crown.

he has come a good distance from the brash and impetuous young man of the first three acts. In the following scene 3 he again reveals his emotional growth by responding to Pembroke's "Sir, sir, impatience hath his privilege" with " 'Tis true, to hurt his master, no man else"—a reply clearly demonstrating insight into his own earlier rashness.

All this prepares for the following scene when, over the body of Arthur, the Bastard makes the first of two major choices between Commodity and Honour. With England invaded, her forces divided and her king ineffectual, it is plainly to his advantage to follow the departed nobles. Yet when he says, "I am amaz'd, methinks, and lose my way/Among the thorns and dangers of this world," his words not only express his present bewilderment but also represent his sudden awareness of the superficiality of his previous ethics. The man of action becomes for an intense moment the man of thought. Shakespeare compresses within the remainder of the Bastard's speech his acceptance of Arthur's claim to the succession, his declaration against John as the man of self-interest, his recognition of England's loss of fortune, and his decision to ally himself, not with John, but with England. In short, the Bastard renounces with evident risk the principle of Commodity and commits himself to the highest form of Honour. By so doing, he becomes morally worthy of the crown.

It is no accident that immediately following the Bastard's speech we are shown (Act V, scene 1) John demonstrating his own moral weaknesses by capitulating to Pandulph and enduring unremarked such hypocritical sarcasm as Pandulph's "But since you are a gentle convertite,/My tongue shall hush again this storm of war." Indeed, far from feeling any sense of mortification, John is overjoyed, rejoicing that the prophecy of his deposition has come true differently than he had thought: "I did suppose it should be on constraint;/But, heaven be thank'd it is but voluntary." By such an act and such rejoicing, John forfeits all moral right to the crown. Not only by the juxtaposition of the two scenes, but also by the disparity of their attitudes within this second scene, the Bastard and John are thrown into dramatic contrast. John's attitude is obvious from, among other things, his choice of pronouns: "Would not *my* lords return to *me* again . . ."; "The legate of the Pope hath been with *me,*/And *I* have made a happy peace with him." The Bastard, on the other hand, speaks only of "us": "Shall *we,* upon the footing of *our* land . . ." (my italics). The absence of any ethical principles in John has resulted in the elevation of self-interest above the good of England. In the moment of crisis John has only himself to rely upon—and his self is a moral vacuum. Still trying to escape, or perhaps still unaware of, moral realities, he degenerates into feeble vacillations. The Bastard, despite his earlier suspicions, is clearly dumbfounded by John's total collapse. When he tries to stir him to action by defining the ideal reactions of a king (lines 43-61), the Bastard is defining himself. When he denounces as "inglorious" the league John has made with Pandulph, his convictions are those of An English King. Finally, when John says weakly, "Have thou the ordering of this present time," his words represent a symbolic relinquishment of the crown to the man who deserves it morally but not legally.

Yet if the Bastard has committed himself to Honour, it is no such ingenuous Honour as that which precipitated Blanche to destruction. It has at least once already withstood the severest inner tests of Commodity, and it has proven shrewdly adept at discerning Commodity in others. When (Act V, scene 2) he berates the French, the Bastard speaks not only as John's surrogate but as the symbol of An English King: "Now hear our English King,/For thus his royalty doth speak in me." The ambiguity of "royalty" is deliberate, for as the son of Richard I the Bastard has some claim to literal truth, and certainly his scornful defiance here by no means mirrors the John for whom he ostensibly speaks. However, the Bastard is not nearly so confident as he makes out; his "brave," as Lewis calls it, should remind us of his satiric deflations of chivalric bravado earlier in the play. What he is doing here, it seems apparent, is turning Commodity against itself, attempting to prevent the possible overthrow of England by deluding the superior French forces into arbitration. In short, he is using the techniques of Commodity in the service of Honour.

The following scene (Act V, scene 3) is particularly noteworthy. The shortest of the entire play, its very brevity calls attention to it as the culmination of a series of continuing contrasts between the Bastard and John. We have just seen the Bastard's shrewd attempt to delude the French with solitary defiance as he plays the symbolic rôle of An English King. Now we are shown John completely incapacitated—not by poison, for he has not yet gone to Swinstead Abbey where the poisoning occurs, but by a fever. The fever, which has troubled him for some time, is less physiological than psychological; it represents perhaps a form of divine punishment for Arthur's death as well as John's unconscious awareness that in moral reality he is no longer king. His symbolic relinquishment of the crown to the Bastard earlier is confirmed by the arrival of a Messenger with the words:

> My lord, your valiant kinsman, Faulconbridge,
> Desires your Majesty to leave the field
> And send him word by me which way you go.

This is not, one notes, the request of a subject, but the order, the "desire," of one who is quite aware of his authority. Nor is John's prompt obedience to be taken lightly; feverish or not, the head of an army does not withdraw from the field without his withdrawal being interpreted as a signal of disaster. But John is only the titular head of England now, and his withdrawal is not in the least damaging; the Bastard remains on the field, clearly in command, and, as Salisbury ruefully remarks, "In spite of spite, alone upholds the day." No sooner does the Bastard "desire" John to leave the field than Fortune turns against the French, for immediately after John acquiesces to the Bastard's order the Messenger adds:

> Be of good comfort; for the great supply
> That was expected by the Dauphin here,
> Are wreck'd three nights ago on Goodwin Sands.

The fact that the supply ships were wrecked "three nights ago" does not alter the fact that Shakespeare chooses to present the information dramatically at this precise point. Later (Act V, scene 5) the same information is reported to Lewis along with the news that "The Count Melun is slain; the English lords/By his persuasion are again fallen off." In short, the ill fortune that has dogged the English since John's decision to murder Arthur (Act III, scene 3) is reversed when the Bastard's symbolic private deposition of John is publicly confirmed by John's departure from the battlefield.

There are two obvious objections to this theory about the change of English fortunes: first, that the return of the English nobles seems more clearly to act as the symbolic cause; and, second, that the Bastard's later loss of his forces in the tides seems to belie the change. The return of the nobles, however, is a matter of simple expediency occasioned by Melun's warning that Lewis intended to execute them if he carried the day. No doubt the nobles have some trace of patriotic sentiment, or, if not that, they must at least realize from the narrowness of their escape that Commodity proves a most unreliable guide to action. However, the fact that before facing John they first ingratiate themselves with the young Prince Henry, who can serve as their intercessor with John, suggests that their interests are not entirely in the welfare of England.

The second objection—that the Bastard's loss of half his army in the Lincoln Washes argues against a change of English fortune—requires that we examine the Bastard's situation at this time. Through the second half of *King John* we have seen him steadily rising towards the station of An English King. In a symbolic sense he has deposed John and successfully led the English armies. With the news that John is dying, then, the opportunity has arisen for him to transform a symbolic kingship into an actual kingship; he has only to forswear Honour. This possibility is tentatively suggested by Hubert when he says (Act V, scene 4):

> I left [John] almost speechless, and broke out
> To acquaint you with this evil, that you might
> The better arm you to the sudden time
> Than if you had at leisure known of this.

Realizing that with the return of the traitorous nobles a power struggle may ensue, Hubert pledges his support to the Bastard. A few lines later, when the Bastard says, not so much to Hubert as to himself, "Withhold thine indignation, mighty heaven,/And tempt us not to bear above our power!" he is speaking not only with reference to the nobles but also with reference to himself, simultaneously acknowledging an impulse to kingship and admitting the dishonourableness of that impulse. As he said a little earlier to Hubert, "I come one way of the Plantagenets," and "one way" is not sufficient to justify an aspiration to the crown. Now, having phrased the alternatives of Honour and Commodity, he is reminded of something by his use of the word *power*. When he adds, "I'll tell thee, Hubert, half my power this night,/Passing these flats, are taken by the tide," he has realized that the loss of his army has personal as well as military implications, that this check of power also represents a form of divine injunction against any attempt to seize power for himself. As in the scene over Arthur's body, he again makes his decision quickly—"conduct me to the King"—and with this decision he again renounces Commodity and redeclares himself for the good of England, thus becoming most worthy of the crown at the moment of rejecting it.

It is, therefore, perfectly appropriate that the Bastard is given the concluding speech of the play, which is usually reserved for the king. He has confirmed his loyalty to England and to the soon-to-be King Henry III in this final scene. Yet this final speech of his, with its conspicuously qualifying "if"—". . . Naught shall make us rue,/If England to itself do rest but true"—is not just a set piece of perfunctory patriotism with which to conclude the play. The Bastard is too perspicacious and he has had too much experience with the renegade nobles not to be suspicious of their professions of Honour in this last scene. His closing speech is both a stirring proclamation of an ideal—but not, he realizes, untempered—national unity, and also his declaration to the nobles of the

standards by which he has been governed and by which he expects them
to be governed in the future. Thus, with what we might call "experienced" Honour dictating the terms to Commodity, *King John* concludes
upon the same theme with which it began.

The Historical Pattern from
Richard the Second to *Henry the Fifth*

by Derek Traversi

Anyone approaching the study of Shakespeare's second, and greater, series of plays on English history must be acutely aware of treading controversial ground. Neither on the guiding conception of the series nor on its artistic merits has agreement been reached, so that spirited defences of the patriotic interpretation—like that put forward in more than one place by Professor J. Dover Wilson[1]—alternate with readings of a very different kind, less simple and positive in tone. The increased attention now given to the background of the plays in terms of contemporary political thought, though in many ways illuminating, has not been without dangers of its own. There is a very real risk that erudition, in relating these plays to their period, may end by obscuring their true individuality, the personal contribution by which they live as works of art. The true artist, when circumstances induce him to approach political conceptions, gives them a new human value in the light of his own experience; and it is this combination of old and new, the inherited theme and its individual re-creation, that confers upon Shakespeare's historical plays their distinctive and transforming interest.

This general observation, which applies in varying degrees to Shakespeare's earlier chronicles,[2] is still more true of the set of plays which,

[1] In *The Fortunes of Falstaff* (Cambridge: The University Press, 1943) and in his introduction to the two *Henry IV* plays and *Henry V* (Cambridge: The University Press, 1946 and 1947).

[2] Professor J. Dover Wilson, following earlier students of the *Henry VI* plays, has defended the view that these represent the reshaping for performance by Shakespeare's own company of plays originally written by other hands; but other investigation, such as that incorporated in Peter Alexander's important study, *Shakespeare's Henry VI and Richard III* (Cambridge: The University Press, 1929), tends to give Shakespeare greater credit for originality in his early writings.

extending from *Richard II* to *Henry V,* represents his most extended treatment of material derived from English history. The starting point of the series is, in accordance with the inherited conception, an adaptation to the exigencies of Tudor political thought of traditional conceptions of monarchy. The royal office is assumed to be divinely instituted, the necessary guarantee of order in a state nationally and patriotically conceived; the political thought expressed in these plays combines the fervent nationalism of the day, fostered for practical ends by the ruling dynasty, with sacramental notions of monarchy more venerable than itself. In the period covered by this series, however, the emphasis rests on the interruption of the relationship which should naturally exist, according to the traditional view, between king and subject, on the disastrous consequences of that interruption, and on the restoration of ordered rule, after the uneasy interim of Henry IV's reign, on a more secure, if more limited, basis under the authority of his son. The relevance to contemporary purposes of the lesson already drawn from the events depicted by such chroniclers as Hall and Holinshed [3] was, beyond doubt, a determining factor in Shakespeare's choice of subject.

As we follow the development of this closely integrated series,[4] we are aware that the historical theme corresponds in its entirety to the plan just indicated. It opens with the overthrow, in *Richard II,* of a king whose hereditary position and claim to allegiance are in themselves unchallenged by a usurper—Bolingbroke—whose action derives from, though it is not excused by, crimes committed and at heart acknowledged by his victim. Chief among these crimes was the murder of Edward III's son, Thomas, Duke of Gloucester, referred to by Shakespeare on several occasions[5] and more directly treated by an unknown writer in the earlier play of *Woodstock.*[6] From the moment of Richard's murder, the royal office, its reputation already tarnished by the unworthiness of its last legitimate holder, ceases to confer upon the king a natural, spontaneous right to allegiance; its necessary authority will be restored, if at all, on the basis of a more conscious, deliberate estimate of political realities, and only after the consequences of the original crime have worked themselves out through the body politic in disintegration and bloodshed.

---

[3] Hall's *Chronicle* was published in 1548, Holinshed's in 1577.

[4] The continuity of the argument does not, of course, imply that the four plays were originally conceived as a single unit, but simply that the later terms of the series recognized the existence of the earlier. In point of fact, some three years separate *Richard II,* which must have been written around 1595, from the two parts of *Henry IV* and *Henry V.*

[5] See more especially *Richard II,* I. ii.   [6] Edited by A. P. Rossiter in 1946.

The fruits of usurpation in terms of civil strife are, indeed, amply shown in the two plays devoted to the usurper's reign. Henry's desire to rule well is countered throughout by the dubious origins of his power. Usurpation breeds rebellion in those who, after all, have only backed his claim for ends of their own, so that the new reign resolves itself into the king's inconclusive struggle against the selfish interests which he has himself fostered to gain access to the throne. This new situation is accompanied by a notable extension of the ground covered by the action. Beyond the remnants of the original feudal relationship between the king and his aristocratic vassals—a relationship which the act of rebellion has subjected to stress, taken out of the natural order of things—the range of political realities covered by these two plays is most notably widened. The political events depicted still take place, in the main, within the aristocratic limits where decisions are arrived at and the course of action determined; but the consequences of this action are expanded—as they never were in *Richard II*—to cover a more ample field. Disorder, no longer confined to the clash of courtly rivalries, spreads from these to cover the nation's life; and this disorder, which breeds within itself an increasingly explicit comment, the repudiation of those whose deeds have opened the way to its tragically conceived effects, is brought home most immediately to the king through the dissolute behaviour of his son.

This dissolution, however, though related to the diseased state of the body politic, is less real than apparent. Hal, brought up in the new order of things, represents rather a fresh beginning than a continuation of the sombre realities around him. It is true that his behaviour in the *Henry IV* plays is conditioned, at least in part, by the nature of the society in which he finds himself; but this situation, which is not of his making, does not weigh upon him with the limiting, constraining force that so imposes itself upon his father. His conduct is marked from the first by a sense that the traditional sanctions of monarchy are no longer immediately valid, that the implications of the royal office need to be reconsidered in a new world of uncertainties. This reconsideration, presented through the successive stages of the action, is a principal theme of the *Henry IV* plays. Hal is subjected to a process of education which finally enables him to assume, with full competence, the burden of authority in the circumstances which his father's act (and Richard's own previous unworthiness) has brought into being; and in this process, his own dispassionate nature, his readiness to see things as they are, plays a decisive part. When, at the end of *Henry IV*, Part II, his growth into responsibility is complete, the entire series is rounded off with the consolidation of a new political order concentrated on the person of Henry V, who possesses to a supreme degree his father's political capacity but whose authority has not been directly flawed by the dubious nature of its origins.

Thus far, the theme followed in this series of plays belongs, in its main outline, to the political commonplaces of Shakespeare's age. The overthrow and restoration of ordered rule under the royal fountainhead of authority are, however, no more than a part—albeit essential—of his purpose. The traditional story presented a further motive for development in the portrayal of Prince Hal, whose progress from dissolute heir apparent to responsible monarch gives a main thread of significant continuity to the series. It is, in fact, through his study of the Prince, and of his relationship to his father, that Shakespeare, by shifting his emphasis from the public to the personal aspect of his story, approaches the full originality of his conception. The question we come increasingly to ask ourselves, as we follow the various stages of the Prince's career, is one which, because it stands in evident relationship to realities in the moral order, has obvious dramatic possibilities: What are the personal, as distinct from the political, qualities that go to the making of a king? The answer is provided in several stages, each of which is at once based on contemporary notions of the political character and vastly extends the implications of these notions, passing from an affirmation of the necessity of monarchy to a searching analysis of the qualities and limitations of the public personality.

The study has been prepared for, mainly in its negative aspects, by the portrayal of Hal's royal predecessors. The failure of Richard, in the opening play, to exercise effectively the legitimate and divinely sanctioned authority which he alone, in the whole series, can indubitably claim, is shown as a reflection of grave personal weakness. This weakness, having precipitated his own tragedy and brought the royal institution into grave crisis, acts in turn as a conditioning factor in all that follows. Richard's fall and the usurpation of Bolingbroke emphasize between them the necessity of the political qualities for the successful exercise of kingship. By his possession of these qualities Bolingbroke justifies, as far as may be, his otherwise indefensible seizure of the crown; and a clear-sighted and dispassionate estimate of the varied motives which accompany the struggle for power, once the foundations of ordered rule have been called into question, is passed on by Bolingbroke as a basic condition of public life to his son.

The true interest of the conception, however, really begins at this point. The contrast with Richard has established, with what has for Prince Hal the validity of an axiom, the relevance of his father's political gifts; but the presentation of Henry's reign, in the two plays which follow, equally stresses its limitations. Henry IV's concentration upon the political aspects of behaviour, having brought him to the throne, leaves him as king with no sufficient substitute for the accepted sanctions of royalty which he has himself, as a usurper, subjected to outrage. These sanctions are founded, in the last analysis, upon personal and therefore human values, which he has neglected at his peril, and which now exact from him an unwilling recognition of which the son, as he approaches his father with increasing intimacy, cannot fail to be aware. The very concentration upon the political virtues that have enabled Henry to press successfully his claim to the throne becomes, once he has been crowned, a limiting factor, a weakness which, as he increasingly stresses it in his exchanges with Hal, is borne with a persistence akin to tragedy upon his son's thoughts.

In the light of these considerations the apparent contradictions which have so often been felt to underlie the presentation of the Prince's character become consistent and comprehensible. Hal, in his characteristically self-conscious aspiration to princely perfection, is less a free agent than the product of the preceding circumstances by which his own reactions have been shaped. He is presented to our consideration, not merely as an individual, but as the member of a family, whose qualities and defects he shares. The very considerable virtues which bring him finally to political success represent, in more aspects than one, the turning to practical account of inherited limitations. As the son of a usurper, Hal is deprived of the sanctions which the traditional monarch derived from unquestioned heredity, sanctions upon which Richard (to return to the starting point of the series, still alive in its later stages) too complacently counted to offset his personal unworthiness. This lack of traditional sanction, which had constituted his father's problem, becomes, in the political order, his opportunity. It enables him to propose to himself with full awareness ends which a traditional ruler can too easily take for granted, reconciling the legitimate authority which (more clearly than his father) he is in a position to exercise, with the insight and political skill needed to maintain it in a world of shifting and often cynical values. From the outset, the supreme quality inherited by Hal from his father and raised by his own practice to new levels of shrewd consistency is *detachment:* a *detachment* from traditional conceptions which he turns into the active intelligence so firmly applied by him to his relatively legitimate situation, but which is at the same time—and to forget this is to fail to respond to the balanced conception of the character—his limitation as a human being.

Once this situation has been grasped in its full subtlety, the process of "conversion" which Shakespeare derived from his sources and which no doubt contributed in no small measure to the popularity of the series is seen in its true light. In a very important sense, there is in Hal's behaviour no true "conversion" at all. The detachment which we have just asserted to be his distinguishing quality, his most important inheritance from his father, determines from the first moment his attitude in the tavern scenes of the two *Henry IV* plays. Whatever his father may fear, Hal is never truly subjected to the vices with which he associates for ends he has deliberately, and with full consciousness, made his own. From the first, he is only waiting the opportune moment for his self-revelation; this is plainly stated in his first soliloquy[7]—in which Shakespeare turns the lack of verisimilitude in his theme into a psychological virtue—and remains, from that moment, a principal key to his behaviour. Falstaff and his companions are, from this point of view, no more than living examples of the consequences of "misrule," of the anarchy which his father's action has, against his own intentions, promoted but which he has never, with his outlook confined as it is to the narrow sphere of courtly intrigue, properly understood. Henry V, unlike Bolingbroke, *will* understand it, because he has surrounded himself with it, has with set purpose gone so far as to *live* it in his own person; but when the time comes for his tavern friends to be discarded, that action will come easily to a man who has from the first declared his intention of turning away from them as soon as he has extracted, from his contact with them and by intimate observation, the knowledge he requires of men as they are, and—further—as soon as this rejection will appear in its full value in the public eye. That this sober estimate of public convenience implies increasingly some lack of human warmth is no doubt true, but it is no more than one example of the crux upon which all that is most personal in Shakespeare's presentation of the character turns.

The stages of Hal's "public" redemption, to which the growing coolness of his relations with Falstaff are a background, are, roughly speaking, two; they correspond with sufficient exactitude to the two plays into which the *Henry IV* action is divided. The core of his successful affirmation, in Part I, as warrior and man of chivalry lies in the conflict between himself and Harry Percy. As a result of this conflict, a new and politically practical virtue asserts itself victoriously over a tarnished and inadequate conception of aristocratic "honour." Once more, the emphasis is placed upon the rise, under the new conditions implied by Bolingbroke's seizure of power, of a fresh and contemporary attitude to politics. Percy's "honour," presented in him as a sincere attribute, is none the less out of touch with the world in which it moves. It is, in its own despite, verbal in

---

[7] *1 Henry IV*, I. ii.

content, unable to offer an adequate alternative to the political manoeu-vrings which it repudiates but which have nevertheless replaced the traditional loyalties to which the leaders of the rebel faction, even as they follow the claims of self-interest, still ostensibly appeal. As such, it stands for an essentially gullible attitude towards life, and Percy him-self, in a world where all affirmations of nobility call for scrutiny, has become the instrument of unworthy designs. Hal's conception of chiv-alry is, by comparison, self-reliant and workaday, conceived not in rhetoric or pride of caste, but in strict relation to the sober and necessary ends he has proposed to himself. At Shrewsbury, a dying tradition, shorn by the impact of new circumstances of the values which had originally justified it, meets a fresh conception of "virtue," founded on a less preju-diced estimate of practical possibilities, of the true nature of man as a political being, and inevitably succumbs. But behind the triumph of this new conception, justified and necessary as it is, there lies, as the fol-lowing action shows, a sense of relativity, of inescapable hollowness.

This sense, indeed, looms increasingly large in *Henry IV*, Part II, where it is projected for Hal no longer in the simple sphere of active self-affirmation, in which he has proved himself strong, but in a more intimate, personal order. Having asserted himself as a modern prince in the exercise of the chivalrous virtues, and so laid the foundation of his future greatness, Hal is now faced with the more arduous necessity of subduing his own will, of making himself the instrument of a con-ception of justice which transcends all personal considerations and upon which his own authority—if it is to receive true acceptance—must rest. At this point he meets, squarely and for the first time, the true impli-cations of his own nature and of the circumstances which have attended his own rise to political efficacy. It is this fact, above all others, which accounts for the notable change in feeling which distinguishes *Henry IV*, Part II, from the preceding play. The shadow of the traditional concep-tion of monarchy, thrust aside by his father in the act of self-assertion which brought him to the crown, returns as the specific personal problem of the son. It is, indeed, the relation between the necessary impersonality of the king, little short of superhuman in its implications, and the self-assertion called for in a complex and shifting world that becomes in increasing measure the key to Hal's character and to the concept of political behaviour sketched in his development. Having overthrown Percy (a relatively simple triumph), the Prince needs—as the last stage in his preparation for kingship—to overcome himself, to attain the impersonality which his great office requires of him; and this is what is implied, against a sombre background of social realities more extensively presented than in the preceding plays, in his final reconciliation with the Lord Chief-Justice. After this alone, Hal—ostensibly at peace with himself, confirmed in the exalted selflessness of his vocation—is ready to be crowned.

From this exposition of the development in Hal of a study of political perfection (perfection, be it stressed once more, which is neither more nor less than political), it emerges that the king can only be understood in relation to the realm over which he exercises his necessary, his indispensable authority. It is indeed the supreme achievement of this series of plays that, as the personal implications of the royal vocation in Hal are progressively unfolded, they are constantly related to the state of an England which at once reflects and conditions the central presentation of royalty. That this should be so is only natural, because—as we have suggested—these plays regard the king as being, by close analogy, the head of his realm, the incarnation of its purpose, and the summit of its accumulated strength. The "moral" regeneration of Hal (which is, as we have seen, rather a growth in political understanding) is operated throughout in relation to the England he will govern; and the result is a picture of notable consistency and depth, in which each new element, as it is introduced into the action, falls into place in a complete and balanced artistic achievement.

Once more, and in accordance with the nature of the entire series, the complete truth emerges in relation to the various stages of the historical pattern. The "viciousness" of Hal's early surroundings and of his unregenerate behaviour (which his own father, with less than complete understanding, accepts at its face value) reflects the disorder which was at once the cause and the result of Bolingbroke's usurpation; the aristocratic intrigues of the rebels, with their disruptive effect upon the unity of the state, find their reflection in the dissolution of the tavern scenes, supremely incarnated in the anarchy of Falstaff. From this disorder the Prince, even as he participates in it, stands aside in detached sufficiency. He deliberately sets himself to study it, to make himself realistically familiar, *on all levels,* with the conditions of his future rule; and the result is that the dramatic action takes shape, round his person, in a world in which Hotspur and Douglas, Falstaff and Bardolph, Poins and Pistol, each alive in his own right, live further as an integral part of the society which it is the king's vocation to mould into an active unity of purpose. It is the breadth of understanding which follows from this conception of his office—the refusal to be limited exclusively to court circles and values—that distinguishes Hal from his father, for whom the royal authority has always been confined in its exercise to the political manipulation of courtly appetites, and who has shown throughout a distinct contempt, related to, but essentially different from, his son's detachment, for everything that may be described as "popular."

In terms of this detachment, at least, the Prince and Falstaff represent contrasted poles, upon whose clash and subsistent interrelation the conception which animates these plays finally turns. To grasp the nature of the link that binds them together in diversity is to penetrate most closely to the central experience of the series. As Hal assumes his royal responsibilities, he inevitably turns away from his companion in dissolution, until the break is consummated in the final rejection.[8] That rejection is, from the point of view of his growth as a public figure, the necessary external consequence of his acceptance of his royal vocation; this requires a visible turning away from the "misrule" which is the supreme enemy of true kingship, and without it his later triumphs would be inconceivable. In *Henry V*, the king, having finally and with complete self-consciousness assumed the barely human responsibilities of his office, is at last able to use the knowledge he has gained of men and affairs to lead a nation from which the figure of "riot" has been finally expelled to his victorious enterprise in France.

The triumph of Henry V, however, though valid in its own right, equally confirms what has been implied by the presentation of his character throughout the series. The loss in human qualities which appears, in these plays, to be involved in the very fact of political success gives a tragic undertone to his triumphant progress. For what is at each stage, and in accordance with the initial conception, a realistic study of social dissolution is turned, by the most daring stroke of all, into a source of comic energy, a comment developed in parallel form upon the entire political action. It is here that the function of Falstaff enters into its full subtlety, combining the vicious rôle of the fat knight as misleader of youth and incarnation of anarchy with that of vivid human commentator on the detached inhumanity which political ability, once the natural bonds of an ordered society have been broken, seems increasingly to imply. This double conception of Falstaff, and its constant relationship to the various stages of the Prince's development is Shakespeare's supreme personal contribution to the historical material of these plays.

From this point of view, again, the Prince's attitude towards Falstaff develops notably in the course of the action. In Part I, as Hal observes in Falstaff the real consequences of anarchy and misrule (consequences which are shown, above all, in the Eastcheap robbery, in which the Prince, albeit in detachment, participates), he is confirmed in his political

---

[8] *2 Henry IV*, v. v.

vocation. At each stage, however, Falstaff provides, besides a living picture of disorder, a valid comic commentary. His function up to the battle of Shrewsbury is evidently in some sense a critical one, not altogether different, though vastly developed, from that of Faulconbridge in *King John*.[9] The Prince's reconciliation with his father is preceded by the parody of that reconciliation in the tavern,[10] in the course of which Falstaff, defending himself against charges which will ultimately prove fatal to him, symbolically assumes the throne of misrule; and the final victory over Hotspur is accompanied by the parody of warlike valour and by an implicit comment on the values of "heroism" itself.[11] In neither case are we to equate mockery simply with seriousness, or parody with truth; but in each an aspect of reality relevant to a balanced judgement is being advanced. The linking through one personage of the serious to the comic action, so that a commentary on the one springs out of the limitation, the stressed corruption of the other, is the most original feature of the whole play.

In Part II, as the Prince directly faces the deeper implications of his vocation, a new and increasingly sombre note is struck in the avowedly comic scenes. Falstaff, in tune with his surroundings, grows notably in age and obvious decay. Losing a great part of the vitality which had distinguished him in the previous play, he becomes subdued to the quality of the life around him, in which senility, disillusionment, and impotence largely predominate. Equally, however, he shows at moments a new kind of tragic pathos which, presented without sentiment, is not incompatible with his growing monstrosity and which even his necessary subjection to justice cannot entirely obscure. His age, accentuating in him the elements of dissolution, also stresses a sense of death which is shared, finally and as one element in a complex effect, by the very order which has seen Henry's rise to power. The picture of an England in disorder, the background to the Prince's growth in political competence, expands from court and tavern, already conceived in parallel function, to include Gloucestershire, the local foundations of life in a rural society; and the sense of age and decay which accompanies this presentation (though it does not exhaust it) is a background to the increasingly sombre quality of Hal's own reflections and to the cynicism which has throughout marked the behaviour of the political leaders to whom success is in the process of becoming an end in itself.

Of the Prince himself we should not say that he is, by the end of the

---

[9] If one aspect of Faulconbridge finds fulfilment in the figure of Edmund in *King Lear*, another can be said to anticipate the comic spirit of Falstaff.

[10] *I Henry IV*, II. iv.   [11] *Ibid.*, v. iv.

series, subdued to this new order of cynicism, against which, indeed, his royal actions are conceived as a decisive reaction. Yet his inevitable relation to this order colours his thought and has from the first conferred a certain sombre detachment from humanity upon his behaviour, which finds its supreme practical expression in the rejection scene (the necessity of which, however, is not in question). It is worth noting that Hal's final assumption of his royal duties is accompanied, as its necessary corollary, not merely by the banishment but by the death of Falstaff, with which the relationship between them concludes. In the double link which, at the heart of an England which these plays have progressively depicted in the widening scope of its varied social relationships, binds Falstaff to Hal as necessary sacrifice and vivid protest opposed to tried virtue and cold competence, we approach the true sense, the final originality, of this great series of plays.

A Little More than a Little

by R. J. Dorius

I

By showing us the power and frailty of seven kings, Shakespeare's nine English history plays (excluding *Henry VIII*) imply a standard of good kingship which no one of his kings, except possibly Henry V, fully attains. Both this standard and Henry's relationship to it have puzzled many commentators, and with good reason, since the great tragedies imply somewhat different standards, with far more emphasis upon heroic action. The tragic hero's willingness to take terrible risks, to throw away power and life itself for a cause, is not demanded of the kings of the histories. By and large, except for Richard III, they are more conservative; their mission is less to question and dare than to reconcile and maintain. They are absorbed less with the state of man than with practical politics; their problem is not why but how. It follows that they cannot risk the "tragic waste" precipitated by the inflexible highminded resolve of the heroes. Indeed, the overweening ambition of a partly tragic character like Hotspur is seen in the context of the histories as slightly comic.

What seems to set off the values of these plays most markedly from those of the tragedies is the importance given by the histories to the virtues of prudence and economy. For in the chronicle plays these are the essential qualities, together with strength of character—kingliness—for a ruler's governance both of himself and his realm. To what degree the importance of these qualities in Shakespeare, up to the turn of the century, is related to the poet's response to crises of his own day, or to the spectacle of an older England wasted for a hundred years through the incompetence or violence of a succession of weaklings, usurpers, and tyrants, it is difficult to say. But it is clear that the fullest exploration

"A Little More than a Little," by R. J. Dorius. From *Shakespeare Quarterly*, XI (1960), 13-26. Reprinted by permission of the author and The Shakespeare Association of America, Inc.

of the significance of prudence and economy in state affairs, and thus also of their opposites—carelessness, excess, waste, and disease, is to be found in the sequence running from *Richard II* through *Henry V*. It is with the development of these themes of good husbandry and extravagance through the metaphoric language of this tetralogy, and especially of *Richard II,* that this paper will be chiefly concerned. The thematic imagery of these plays possesses a logic and coherence striking enough to justify numerous comparisons between images of different dramas and the assumption that the group forms, in essential features, if not perhaps in initial conception or over-all effect, a unified design.

From Richard's "I wasted time, and now doth time waste me" at the beginning of the series to Henry V's weighing time "Even to the utmost grain" at the end, a concept of good husbandry presides like a goddess over the turbulent experiences of these plays. The assumption behind this emphasis upon watchful economy seems to be that life and power are precious gifts and that to squander them or to misdirect them is a crime against God and the state. And to be careless is to hand one's life and throne over to the initiative of others, who may turn both to their own ends. A negligent and heedless prince, like Richard II, creates a vacuum of power which must be filled, and invites disaster. Throughout, waste or destruction is associated in these plays with an apparently antithetical theme—fatness or excessive growth. Both are the extremes of which economy is the mean, or the ends to which extravagance in man or government might lead. We frequently find in these plays a kind of logical or psychological relationship between the stages of a process from health to disease, marked by metaphors depicting carelessness, eating or sleeping, deafness or blindness, rioting, fatness or excess, sickness, waste, barrenness, and death. The general movement of *Richard II* and of the cycle through 2 *Henry IV* is from youthful or springtime luxuriance to aged or wintry barrenness. Of course these polarities are developed more fully in the later Shakespeare. But the well-known association in the great tragedies between images of excess or disease and faults ranging from mere folly to crime is already fully developed in these histories. The significance of Hamlet's dark reference to the world as "an unweeded garden/That grows to seed" and to man as a beast whose chief good is "but to sleep and feed" is greatly heightened if seen through the preoccupation with things gross in nature and men in the English histories.

The collaboration of plot, character, and thematic imagery to create a unity of tone and meaning is so intimate in these plays that a word or metaphor can be said to be deepened into character or extended into plot. Thus in *Henry IV* the pervasive imagery of extremes is in a sense embodied both in a lean king of state literally worn away with anxiety and in a fat king of revels surrounded by slivers of himself, "Pharaoh's lean kine." Shape is at least partly an index to character. Everywhere the ideal king, the "figure of God's majesty," is contrasted with the "ugly form/Of base and bloody insurrection. . . ." [1] Frequently fast follows feast, early death follows premature growth, in emphatic contrast. In the theatre, the sickness of the divided commonwealth is visibly present in the range of physical proportions of the characters on the stage. In Part II (III. i), the spectacle of the harassed lonely king watching through the night is preceded by the convivial brawling involving fat Saturn and Tearsheet-Venus "in conjunction" and followed by the pricking of the ragamuffins, as Falstaff misuses the king's press. It is almost as though these wastrels, like the crown itself, were, as the Prince says, feeding "upon the body of my father" (IV. v. 160).

The most important antitheses in the histories are often sharpened by what appear to be minor tricks of language. The merry word-games in which the Prince and Falstaff engage, the matchings of "unsavory similes" of fatness and thinness, represent a comic playing with political and moral themes at the core of these plays. One of Falstaff's favorite puns points up the connection between waste and fatness. "Your means are very slender, and your waste is great," says the Chief Justice, posed against Falstaff at the beginning of Part II, and Falstaff replies, "I would my means were greater and my waist slenderer" (I. ii. 160-163). Tagged as Sir John Paunch by Hal, Falstaff rejoins, "Indeed, I am not John of Gaunt, your grandfather . . ." (I:II. ii. 70-71). What begins in a word or name can come to suggest a way of life. One of the polar oppositions to the careless John who sleeps upon benches afternoons and has the "disease of not list'ning" (II:I. ii. 138) is this care-worn John who puns on his own name before Richard II:

> For sleeping England long time have I watch'd;
> Watching breeds leanness, leanness is all gaunt.
>
> [II. i. 77-78]

We usually find in the histories that the responsible man and state are thin, the heedless usually fat. Honor-seeking Hotspur, "Amongst a grove the very straightest plant," can be contrasted not only with Falstaff, "out of all order, out of all compass," who reduces honor to a word, but with Richard II, who stoops "with oppression" of the "prodigal

---

[1] References to Part 2 of *Henry IV* are indicated thus: II:IV.i.39-40. All readings are from the *Complete Works,* edited by G. L. Kittredge, Boston, 1936.

weight" of his nobles. Indeed, imagery of over-eating is applied both to the rightful ruler and the usurper, as the sickness of the head of the state develops. From Gaunt's remark about the "eager feeding" which "doth choke the feeder," young Richard (II. i. 37), to Worcester's criticism in *Henry IV* of the lean king who once set out to purge the state of its excesses, is in many ways a single movement. Henry IV, made "portly" by the help of the Percies,

> did oppress our nest;
> Grew by our feeding to so great a bulk
> That even our love durst not come near your sight
> For fear of swallowing. . . .
>
> [I:V. i. 61-64]

The eaters are eaten and the would-be physicians become centers of contagion. The lean may wax and the fat wane, but all go to extremes. Henry IV speaks what might be the motto of the histories: "a little/More than a little is by much too much" (I:III. ii. 72-73). Implicit everywhere is the unrealized possibility in both man and state of a kind of Aristotelian norm, an ideal of moderation or of equilibrium among opposing forces.

As these quotations have shown, images from the contemporary psychology of the humors help to shape the larger conceptual framework of these plays. The centrality of these metaphors is suggested by the frequency with which characters who fulfill at times a choral role employ them. It is but a step from fatness to disease. Occasionally rising toward the end of his life above his absorption in self-pity, Richard prophesies a growing sickness he failed to cure when he was himself king: the time will come that "foul sin gathering head/Shall break into corruption" (V. i. 58-59). Meanwhile, as in *Hamlet* (III. iv. 148-149), "rank corruption, mining all within,/Infects unseen," and the infection spreads before it is finally lanced. Henry IV, like Richard before him, becomes increasingly a helpless observer of a malady he cannot cure:

> Then you perceive the body of our kingdom,
> How foul it is; what rank diseases grow,
> And with what danger, near the heart of it.
>
> [II:III. i. 38-40]

Henry at least faces more frankly than Richard the fact that he himself is the sick heart. In Part II, the Archbishop, though a rebel, maintains a very detached attitude toward the civil war. He speaks of the discontent following the supplanting of Richard by Bolingbroke as a sickness of the "beastly feeder," the people themselves, who are like dogs that alternately sate themselves and "disgorge" successive kings: "The commonwealth is sick of their own choice;/Their over-greedy love hath surfeited" (II. iii. 87-88). Later he includes two reigns and both royalists and rebels in a general indictment:

> we are all diseas'd
> And with our surfeiting and wanton hours
> Have brought ourselves into a burning fever,
> And we must bleed for it; of which disease
> Our late King, Richard, being infected, died.
>
> [II:IV. i. 54-58]

And, though he disclaims it, he also tries to become England's physician,

> To diet rank minds sick of happiness
> And purge the obstructions which begin to stop
> Our very veins of life.

"Surfeiting" and "wanton" are above all the words for Richard II. The disease which begins in the mind of this king spreads to the body of the state and to its noblemen, and the judicious bleeding and purging of England are delayed throughout three plays, until the "mood" (and "mode") is changed, and the "soil" of Henry IV's dubious achievement goes with him into the earth (II:IV. v. 190-200). To trace this creeping infection to its source, a closer analysis of related themes in *Richard II* is now in order.

II

Themes of negligence, excess, and waste are developed in *Richard II* primarily through several strands of imagery—those of time, the garden and sickness, and the farm and death. All are interrelated in a play whose poetic unity has in the last decade been demonstrated many times. When Richard, the state's timekeeper, threatens to appropriate the titles and property which banished Bolingbroke should inherit from John of Gaunt, York sternly equates the rights of inheritance with cosmic law:

> Take Hereford's rights away, and take from Time
> His charters and his customary rights;
> Let not to-morrow then ensue to-day;
> Be not thyself—for how art thou a king
> But by fair sequence and succession?
>
> [II. i. 195-199]

To interrupt the succession of father to son is to endanger the blood descent from king to king, even to un-king a rightful sovereign. It is to question the very foundations of what the Gardener (in III.iv) calls "law and form and due proportion," to make time itself have a stop. The suggestion is that "Time" draws up all charters and alone gives them meaning. Within forty lines of this warning we learn that the king is indeed not himself, but "basely led/By flatterers . . . ," and within a hundred that the discontented nobles have decided to seize the time to "make high majesty look like itself. . . ." Bolingbroke is later accused of having returned to England "Before the expiration of thy time" (the prescribed six years of banishment), and of taking "advantage of the absent time." But Richard's time is "absent" less because he is away in Ireland when Bolingbroke returns than because he has failed to act promptly within it and has abused it. And yet the usurper compounds Richard's crimes. Confronted by the king's loyal friends, Bolingbroke claims "I am a subject,/And I challenge law" (II. iii. 133-134). York's reply, however, suggests that Hereford is plucking or seizing (the play's words for the usurper) for his own ends the law and time ignored by Richard. York has had a "feeling" for the injury done Bolingbroke,

> But in this kind to come, in braving arms,
> Be his own carver and cut out his way
> To find out right with wrong—it may not be. . . .
>
> [II. iii. 141-145]

Since Richard is himself, as we soon see, a far more clumsy "carver," he is soon cut out of both kingship and kingdom. In the exacting world of the histories, to lose the initiative—or even to act prematurely, like Hotspur—may be to lose one's life. Bolingbroke is above all a master of timing.

Richard dismisses his own folly by invoking divine right. And when he returns from Ireland, the Bishop of Carlisle succinctly phrases the dilemma of the king's taking action:

> Fear not, my lord. That Power that made you king
> Hath power to keep you king in spite of all.
> The means that heaven yields must be embrac'd,
> And not neglected. . . .

If he remains king "in spite of all," Richard surely has no need to rouse himself against the enemy. This doubleness of attitude deeply penetrates the play, for images of inexorability, like those of the rising and falling sun or buckets or of Fortune's wheel, are everywhere contrasted with less fatalistic images of medicine and growth. For nearly two hundred lines at the center of the play, as Richard learns piecemeal that soldiers, subjects, nobles, and favorites have left him, he veers between an exultant characterization of himself as the "Searching eye of heaven" that leaves the guilty "trembling at themselves" (36-62) and a cry of despair: "All souls that will be safe, fly from my side;/For time hath set a blot upon my pride" (80-81). He blames the "time," which, like his nobles, the "unruly jades," he could not "manage."

That he himself has abused time Richard finally sees with unusual objectivity in Act V when he is alone in Pomfret:

> How sour sweet music is
> When time is broke and no proportion kept . . . !
> And here have I the daintiness of ear
> To check time broke in a disordered string;
> But, for the concord of my state and time,
> Had not an ear to hear my true time broke.
> I wasted time, and now doth time waste me. . . .
>
> [V. v. 42-49]

Few of the kings of the histories have the dainty ear to match royal decree with external event, neither anticipating nor delaying. Dying Gaunt had hoped that his advice to Richard would "Enforce attention like deep harmony," but York said that Richard's ears were "stopp'd" with flattery. And, opposing deafening "will" to listening "wit," York implied that Richard was out of step with kingdom and self: "all too late comes counsel to be heard/Where will doth mutiny with wit's regard" (II.i.27-28). Richard's inner mutiny renders him unable to maintain the "concord of my state and time," and he falls from wilfulness to willessness when first affrighted. Like several other crises in these plays, this fall is enacted simultaneously on the level of plot, character, and language. In the theatre, in the solemn descent from Flint Castle in Act III, stage setting and movement are extensions of verbal imagery. And at Westminster in Act IV Richard's ritualistic speeches and his gestures un·kinging himself celebrate, as has been pointed out, a kind of inverse coronation. Incapable of setting firmly the pace of England's affairs, Richard must eventually dance to another's tune. The king who cannot keep time is doomed at the end of the play to become a timepiece: "my time/Runs posting on in Bolingbroke's proud joy,/While I stand fooling here, his Jack o' th' clock" (V.v.58-60). And in an elaborately formal figure, the monarch who faced many follies and, finally outfaced, shatters his mirrored visage at Westminster, reduces himself to a mere clockface, time's "numb'ring clock." Though it has received little attention, the imagery of time is developed and resolved as satisfyingly in Shakespeare's plotting of Richard's decline and fall as the more famous imagery of the sun, which characterizes the sun king's defeat in his pathetic wish: "O that I were a mockery king of snow,/Standing before the sun of Boling-broke . . ." (IV.i.260-261).

Richard's time is "broke" at the very beginning of the play, and his early folly is also depicted in related images of gardening and sickness. Though the parallels between Richard as gardener and king are developed fully only in the last scene of Act III, they are central to the meaning of the entire drama. The Gardener tells us that Richard, like a careful Adam, should have pruned his garden or state in the spring. The gardeners themselves

> at time of year
> Do wound the bark, the skin of our fruit trees,
> Lest, being over-proud in sap and blood,
> With too much riches it confound itself.
>
> [III. iv. 57-60]

The moral of this prudence is pointed up yet more crisply in an allied image from an earlier play. In *2 Henry VI*, Queen Margaret warns Henry of the ambitions of Humphrey of Gloucester:

> Now 'tis the spring, and weeds are shallow-rooted.
> Suffer them now, and they'll o'ergrow the garden
> And choke the herbs for want of husbandry.
>
> [III. i. 31-33]

We are reminded of the ancient tithe exacted for God or king at harvest time, as though abundance would breed pride and consequent guilt.

Waste and ruin, apparently, are not only the result of human folly but the inevitable outcome of any undisciplined process of nature. Things in a natural state grow too much, and weeds and nobles must be trimmed. But heedless Richard is swarming with caterpillars. One implication of these passages is that a good king must improve on nature by protecting living things (especially himself) against their own excesses. And he must foresee trouble and take his stitch in time. Government demands perpetual wakefulness.

Careless Richard has "suffer'd" a "disordered spring." He has failed to "Cut off the heads of too fast growing sprays/That look too lofty in our commonwealth" (III.iv.34-35). And he has neglected to "root away/The noisome weeds" and to trim judiciously: "Superfluous branches/We lop away, that bearing boughs may live" (63-64). The thinly disguised political allegory of the garden scene scarcely succeeds in making these remarkable active verbs—"wound," "Cut off," "root away," and "lop away" (when applied to "great and growing men")—very palatable to the modern reader. But Shakespeare takes his often daring analogues between the king, the state, and external nature as seriously here as in the major tragedies, which imply a very different ethic. The Gardener, whose formal speech suggests that he has a choral function as a kind of alter-ego for Richard, states that Richard should have acted "like an executioner," for now "our sea-walled garden, the whole land,/Is full of weeds, her fairest flowers chok'd up . . ." (43-44). But at the very beginning of the play, the sternness of this duty of the king is contrasted sharply with Richard's indecisiveness. Richard there attempts to resolve the "swelling difference" between Bolingbroke and Mowbray, not by the "Justice" of a traditional duel, but by banishment. At first, as the blank verse of the first scene shifts suddenly into rhyme, he chants

> Let's purge this choler without letting blood.
> This we prescribe, though no physician;
> Deep malice makes too deep incision.
> Forget, forgive; conclude and be agreed;
> Our doctors say this is no month to bleed.
>
> [153-157]

Like a physician maintaining a balance among the body's humors, however, Richard should promptly have made a "deep incision" to "purge" blood overproud and too rich, just as the precautionary Gardener wounds the bark of his fruit trees. The parallel is explicit: tapping is bleeding, and both as gardener and as doctor Richard is negligent. Even Gaunt's solicitations for his son fail to account fully for Richard's stopping of the duel at Coventry in the third scene, "for," as Richard says, "our eyes do hate the dire aspect/Of civil wounds plough'd up with neighbors' sword . . ." (127-128). This is the moment to "check time broke" and the "too fast growing sprays," but Richard is not listening.

That Richard's eyes have not always hated civil wounds is made clear in the somber colloquy which takes place between these first and third scenes of chivalric challenging. Here the Duchess of Gloucester tells us of Richard's hand in the death of his uncle Woodstock, who was "crack'd, and all the precious liquor spilt . . . By envy's hand and murder's bloody axe" (19, 21). And old Gaunt, recalling this political murder later, asks Richard not to spare the blood which they all derive from Edward III: "That blood already, like the pelican,/Hast thou tapp'd out and drunkenly carous'd" (II.i.126-127). Richard has failed to bleed when he should and has tapped and drunk the family blood he should have preserved. Had he bled the "great and growing men" in time, the Gardener tells us, "They might have liv'd to bear, and he to taste/Their fruits of duty" (III.iv.62-63). But there is neither healthy bearing nor fruit in Richard's garden; his land has no "hope to grow" (III.ii.212). And his successor, who greatly exceeds Richard's crimes by plucking out a king "planted many years" and by "grafting" new plants, reaps a "field of Golgotha and dead men's skulls" (IV.i.144).

In still other closely related groups of images, Richard's garden becomes a farm and his land his deathbed. In Gaunt's most famous speech and in several passages on divine right, the play gives us two of the most exalted pictures of England and the divinity of kingship in Shakespeare. But by Act II both have fallen from high estate. Gaunt proceeds from his praise of "This other Eden, demi-paradise," to a terrible indictment. "This blessed plot" is "now leas'd out . . . Like to a tenement or pelting farm" (II.i.59-60).[2] It is bound in not with the "triumphant sea," which keeps it from "infection," but with "inky blots and rotten parchment bonds," and thus the conqueror of others "Hath made a shameful conquest of itself" (64, 66). The "customary rights" of time have become opportunistic "parchment bonds," and Richard robs his land as he robs his cousin. Gaunt is eloquent about the crime of turning a royal realm into real estate: "Why, cousin, wert thou regent of the world,/It were

---

[2] In his suggestive edition of *Woodstock* (London, 1946), A. P. Rossiter points out that Shakespeare not only carries over word for word many of these charges from the earlier play, but takes "as read" in *Woodstock* a complicity with Mowbray in Gloucester's death which weakens Richard's judgment of the contest in Act I. See pp. 47-53, 198, 225-226. What is important here is that Shakespeare fully integrates what he borrows from this and other sources.

a shame to let this land by lease . . ." (109-110). As the demi-paradise becomes a farm, the king becomes a mere overlord: "Landlord of England art thou now, not King./Thy state of law is bondslave to the law . . ." (113-114). This businessman is a far cry from the "deputy elected by the Lord," whom Richard later says the "breath of worldly men cannot depose . . ." (III.ii.56-57). When the shrill chorus of nobles denounces Richard's commercial exploitation of a sacred trust, we are reminded of the threat to the state in *1 Henry IV* when the rebels propose to divide England or of Lear's "darker purpose" in dividing his kingdom. "The King's grown bankrout, like a broken man," the nobles cry, and "Reproach and dissolution hangeth over him" (II.i.257-258). In ravaging his realm Richard is ravaging his subjects: "The commons hath he pill'd with grievous taxes/And quite lost their hearts . . ." (246-247). And the old word "pill'd" (stripped bare, peeled) leads us to the central group of metaphors in which Richard is seen as destroying himself.

The Gardener speaks of the "wholesome herbs/Swarming with caterpillars," and in one of the speeches in the play which unite several of its major strands of imagery, Gaunt identifies the sickness of the king with that of his land. In metaphors like these, perhaps for the first time, Shakespeare has brought the chronicle of a king and of his kingdom into perfect unity.

> Thy deathbed is no lesser than thy land,
> Wherein thou liest in reputation sick. . . .
>
> [II. i. 95-96]

The doctor who should be bleeding the sick body of the realm is himself laid out sick upon it, at the mercy of the physicians who "first wounded" him.

> A thousand flatterers sit within thy crown,
> Whose compass is no bigger than thy head;
> And yet, incaged in so small a verge,
> The waste is no whit lesser than thy land.
>
> [100-103]

The waste (waist) of the king's "Controlling majesty" is the waste of the state. The caterpillars (an Elizabethan commonplace for flattering parasites like Bushy and company), by eating away Richard's power to govern, are devouring the green garden of England. In a similar metaphor, Richard himself later sees his crown as his court, destroyed by idle courtiers. The decline of crown, court, and land is simultaneous. But, unwilling to admit that his principal enemy is his own indulgence, represented by his minions, Richard extravagantly views his real opponent as death, who is merely marking time until he strikes. This illusion is developed in several remarkable figures.

Even before he meets Bolingbroke at Flint Castle, Richard—projecting his own faults, perhaps, and posing them as an implacable abstract enemy—gives us his own version of Gaunt's deathbed warning: "within the hollow crown/That rounds the mortal temples of a king/Keeps Death his court . . ." (III.ii.160-162). The folly Richard has not governed is personified and seen as governing him. Death allows the king to "monarchize" and infuses him with conceit, as if flesh were

> brass impregnable; and humour'd thus,
> Comes at the last, and with a little pin
> Bores through his castle wall, and farewell king!
>
> [168-170]

These images parallel the Gardener's, of Richard as a tree in England's garden, surrounded by "weeds which his broad-spreading leaves did shelter,/That seem'd in eating him to hold him up . . ." (III.ii.50-51). The "sea-walled garden" of Gaunt's speech and the Gardener's, the "flinty ribs" of Flint and Pomfret, and even the divinity that hedges kings cannot defend against himself the guilty monarch who "With nothing shall be pleas'd till he be eas'd/With being nothing" (V.v.40-41). Self-pitying Richard rarely associates his own suffering of the weeds with the doom he views as inexorable. In this respect and others he lacks the stature of the later tragic heroes. Rationalizing the effects of his negligence as necessity, Richard perhaps sees himself, the physician, dieted and bled by death. He implies that he could confront the sword of Bolingbroke, but is clearly helpless before the "little pin." "Subjected thus," Richard cries, "How can you say to me I am a king?" (III.ii.176-177). On his way to the Tower after he is deposed, he tells the queen, "I am sworn brother, sweet,/To grim Necessity, and he and I/Will keep a league till death" (V.i.20-22). This is divine right turned strangely upside down: can't be deposed becomes must be. But there are several indications in the play that Richard cannot really believe in this right, in himself, or in his kingdom.

Bolingbroke crisply observes after Richard has lost power that the shadow of Richard's sorrow has destroyed the shadow of his face. He thereby emphasizes the unreal character of both the kingly fears and the fair "show" of the man who "looks" like a king (III.iii.68-71). Richard's world as king is as fanciful as the thoughts which people his "little world" when he is alone in Pomfret. The weeds and caterpillars which begin to "eat" him are like the generations of "still-breeding thoughts" (IV.v.8) in his head, for both breed only destruction. In one sense, Richard himself is probably Death, tapping out with a little pin the life he cannot govern. The actual threats to the state seem half-shaped by the sick fears of the king, and its later crises partly mirror his fall within his own mind from false security to helpless self-division. This play, dominated by the imagery of excess, presents in its central character a man who turns from an extreme of posturing bravado to passive weeping and finds no kingly norm between. He leaves the seat of a kingdom to "sit upon the ground/And tell sad stories of the death of kings" (III.ii.155-156). He abandons a land "Dear for her reputation through the world" for a "little little grave, an obscure grave," and he becomes his own "tomb." In the language of the play, Richard "melts" away, and we recall Gaunt's stern warning: "Light vanity, insatiate cormorant,/Consuming means, soon preys upon itself" (II.i.38-39).

III

Richard's failure as watchful gardener and physician bequeaths to his successor a realm fat and very sick. The grieving queen suggests an intimate cause-and-effect relationship between the two reigns when she fancies herself giving birth to Bolingbroke, her "sorrow's dismal heir" (II.ii.62), almost as though he were begotten by Richard's folly. But the play's poetic justice is not so simple. Bolingbroke's watchful shrewdness collaborates with Richard's ineffectuality to turn Fortune's wheel. The two men, like other protagonists in Shakespeare, are functions of each other and of their total situation. They are locked in a grim dance in which Richard's weakness opens the way to power for Bolingbroke, and Bolingbroke's silent strength matches Richard's expectations of annihilation. Metaphors of water and of moving buckets suggest a Bolingbroke on high poised and ready to flood a royal reservoir that empties itself. But judgments in the later histories are kinder to the wastrel Richard than to the politician Bolingbroke, whose usurpation and killing of a king are thought more heinous than all of Richard's folly. Though a trimmer, Bolingbroke cannot weed his own garden, for his foes are "enrooted with his friends . . ." (II:IV.i.207). In a long speech to Prince Hal in *1 Henry IV*, troubled Henry sees Richard's blind rioting recapitulated in his son, perhaps as a punishment for Henry's own "mistreadings." This comparison between Richard and Hal affords us a convenient vantage point for pursuing thematic imagery of waste and excess through succeeding plays of this group. Analysis will be centered upon three or four critical passages and the character of Falstaff.

After the excesses of Richard's reign, the Lancastrians reject fatness and imprudence in both man and commonwealth. This rejection underlies the famous first interview of Henry with his son, the Prince's first soliloquy, and the Prince's later banishment of Falstaff. Henry tells Hal that when when he himself courted the crown, his own state, "Seldom but sumptuous, show'd like a feast/And won by rareness such solemnity" (III.ii.57-59). The politician's view of public appearance as strategy could scarcely be further refined. In sixty-odd lines, Henry employs "seldom" three times to refer to his activities and reenforces it with a dozen other words suggesting economy. In a score of very different terms, however, Henry says that men were with King Richard's presence "glutted, gorg'd, and full," for he,

> being daily swallowed by men's eyes,
> They surfeited with honey and began
> To loathe the taste of sweetness. . . .
>
> [70-72, 84]

Kingship is here a kind of candy which should be given the people infrequently, probably when one wishes something from them. Three of Henry's verbs are especially significant:

> And then I stole all courtesy from heaven,
> And dress'd myself in such humility
> That I did pluck allegiance from men's hearts. . . .
>
> [50-52]

It is unnecessary to apply these words to Hal to observe that his seldomness (and his careful "dress") has something in common with that of his father. Indeed, as prince (though not as king), his seldom-acting in the interests of the state is rather like Henry's seldom-appearing, but it commits him to greater personal risks.

Though Hal spends his youth as a madcap of "unyok'd humour" desiring small beer and as a friend of the "trunk of humours," he seems to know from the beginning what he is doing. In his first soliloquy (I.ii.219-241) he exhibits the theatrical sense of timing of other Shakespearian heroes, sharpened to a remarkable degree. He says he will "imitate the sun" which "doth permit" the clouds to "smother up his beauty," so that

his eventual shining will be "more wonder'd at." One of his figures about
holidays employs his father's terms: "when they seldom come, they
wish'd-for come,/And nothing pleaseth but rare accidents." He wants his
reformation to "show more goodly and attract more eyes/Than that
which hath no foil to set it off." This is surely the returning prodigal
calculating every effect: he will "offend to make offence a skill." Part of
this attitude derives from the emphasis upon absoluteness in the heroic
code, according to which it is no "sin to covet honor," and "Two stars"
cannot "share" in glory (I:V.iv.64-65). It derives also from the necessity
of the protagonist in Shakespeare to have a "dainty" ear, from his necessity to collaborate in the nick of time with his fate: "the readiness is
all." "Percy is but my factor . . . ," the Prince tells his father,

> To engross up glorious deeds on my behalf;
> And I will call him to so strict account
> That he shall render every glory up. . . .
>
> [I:III. ii. 147-150]

Bolingbroke's earlier imagery of "more" and "less" here becomes finan-
cial. This young accountant will appear to be eating and sleeping, but
when Hotspur's bond of honor has matured, Hal will spring to life and
exact both principal and interest, "Or I will tear the reckoning from his
heart" (152). Behind this ferocity of course lies the ancient notion of the
conqueror's (like the cannibal's) gaining the strength and virtue of the
conquered. But the Prince's accounting reminds us of the very different
"trim reckoning" by which Falstaff reduces honor to a word, and we
must turn to the knight who only reckons his sack to understand more
fully why the Prince seems to be eating his cake and having it too.

When Henry V banishes the "tutor and the feeder of my riots" at the
end of Part II, he speaks of his companionship with Falstaff as a "dream,"
which—"being awak'd" and watching for sleeping England—he now
despises (II:V.v.53-55). The younger Henry apparently dreams of Falstaff
as Richard II seemed to dream of Bolingbroke in England's garden, but
unlike Richard, he does not succumb to his nightmare. Some critics have
been offended by an image (among others) from Henry's rejection speech
which the metaphors we have been following should help to deepen and
justify: "Make less thy body, hence, and more thy grace;/Leave gor-
mandizing" (56-57). To throw these words and this controversial scene
into larger perspective, we must give appropriate emphasis to the virtues
of law and order embodied in the Chief Justice and of prudence and
economy running through all of the histories. And we must remember

the surprising seriousness with which Falstaff defends himself and the Prince promises to banish him ("I do, I will") during the mock interview —really the trial of a way of life—in Part I (II.iv.462-528). Both seem to know from the beginning that this dream will end. But the complexity of Falstaff and of our attitudes toward him is the best measure of the delicate balance among political and moral attitudes maintained throughout these plays.

The sympathy of the world has always been with the fat knight, and the popularity of these plays would be vastly reduced if, unimaginably, he were not in them. The Prince's turning from "plump Jack," "All the world," can be seen as the rejection of fuller life in favor of power, of being for becoming. That Jack is perhaps an inevitable companion for the Prince, Henry IV makes plain when he associates fatness with nobility in speaking of his son: "Most subject is the fattest soil to weeds;/And he, the noble image of my youth,/Is overspread with them" (II:IV.iv.54-56). But in a comic but highly significant defense of the medicine he recommends for every illness, Falstaff says that the royal blood or soil in Hal was originally "lean, sterile, and bare" and had to be "manured, husbanded, and till'd" with "fertile sherris" to make Hal "valiant" (II:IV. iii. 92-135). Falstaff's phenomenal attractiveness and his mockery of honor and all state affairs give us, among other things, just the insight we need into the "cold blood" of the Lancasters, and also into the dying chivalric code for which his "catechism" (I:V.i.128-140) is a kind of epitaph or *reductio ad absurdum*. But the parallels between the sustained imagery we have been following and Shakespeare's characterization of Falstaff emphasize a darker side of this hill of flesh and illuminate his profoundly functional role in this entire cycle of plays.

Far from threatening the structure of the histories, as some have maintained, Falstaff is one of their central organizing symbols. It is tempting to guess that Shakespeare rapidly found the imagery drawn from nature and animal life which is so marked a feature of the style of *Henry VI* and, far more subtly and intricately, of *Richard II*, inadequate for his increasingly complicated meanings. However we account for it, he developed or chanced upon another and far more expressive vehicle for the ideas of the sick state and king associated in *Richard II* with the overgrown garden. The final evolution of the metaphor of the fat garden and of the sick body politic is probably the fat man. Metaphors from the unweeded garden may underline or even symbolize the sickness of the realm, to be sure, but the tun of man can also, if as alert and witty as Falstaff, make the best possible case for fatness, for the "sin" of being "old and merry," for "instinct" and life rather than grinning honor and death. And he can afford us the point of view from which thinness and economy can be seen as inadequate or unpleasant characteristics. Thus he can throw into clearer relief the entire political and personal ethic of the histories. If we compare the relatively simple equivalence between the physical ugliness of the "elvishmark'd, abortive, rooting hog," Richard III, and the disordered state, on the one hand, with the ambivalent richness of the relationships between the "shapes" of Falstaff and rebellious England, on the other, we can have a helpful index of the deepening of Shakespeare's thought and his growing mastery of his medium over the five or six years (1592-3 to 1597-8) that separate the first of the major histories from the greatest.

Falstaff, then, is both the sickness of the state, the prince of the caterpillars preying on the commonwealth, and the remedy for some of its ills. And his role dramatizes the gulf between the essential virtues of the private man and those of the ruler, for we see in *Antony*, the feast which nourishes the one often sickens the other. Timeless Falstaff is in a curiously reciprocal relationship with time-serving Henry IV, for they are the principal competitors for the Prince's allegiance, in affording by precept and example radically contrasting mirrors for the young magistrate. But the usurper who disdained to follow the example of rioting Richard, as we have seen, finds his eldest son rioting with Falstaff—a kind of embodiment of Henry's inability to weed his own garden. Both the politician and the reveler must disappear from the world of young Henry V before he can find his own voice somewhere between them. He had to befriend Falstaff to know this man's gifts and "language," and in the "perfectness of time" he had to act to arrest the threat of such "gross terms" to the kingdom (II:IV.iv.68-75). The threat is real, for Falstaff is almost the result of a process similar to that referred to by the Archbishop in defending the rebels in Part II: "The time misord'red doth, in common sense,/Crowd us and crush us to this monstrous form. . . ." (II:IV.ii.33-34). We can hardly sentimentalize a Falstaff who says he will "turn diseases to commodity" (II:I.ii.277), when we remember the Bastard's great attack upon "commodity" (opportunism, time-serving) in the nearly contemporary *King John*.[3] And we cannot ignore the outrageousness of Falstaff's cry upon hearing of Hal's succession, just before he himself is banished: "Let us take any man's horses; the laws of England

---

[3] As has frequently been observed, the Falstaff of Part II is a less complicated and attractive figure than the Falstaff of Part I. Increasingly obsessed with his age, his aches and diseases, and, being rarely in the company of the Prince, at once more arrogant and less witty, he seems to embody less of the high-spiritedness which the Lancastrians lack and more of the corruption which threatens to engulf the kingdom.

are at my commandment" (II:V.iii.141-142). Falstaff threatens to usurp the "customary rights" of time, governed as he says he is only by the moon, and to make the law "bondslave" to lawlessness.

Falstaff is depicted in language very similar to that employed in two of the most vivid pictures of disorder in all of Shakespeare, both of them from *2 Henry IV*. Once in a kind of mock despair, the wily Northumberland prays that "order die!/And let this world no longer be a stage/To feed contention in a ling'ring act . . ." (I.i.154-156). Later, the dying king, apprehensive lest his realm receive the "scum" of "neighbour confines" and become a "wilderness," fears that Hal will

> Pluck down my officers, break my decrees;
> For now a time is come to mock at form.
> Harry the Fifth is crown'd. Up, vanity . . . !
> For the Fifth Harry from curb'd license plucks
> The muzzle of restraint, and the wild dog
> Shall flesh his tooth on every innocent.
>
> [IV. v. 118-120, 131-133]

The formless man, "vanity in years," who has mocked at all forms of honor has been the prince's closest companion, potentially a powerful voice in state affairs. The real target of the "fool and jester" has been the "rusty curb of old father antic the law" (I:I.ii.69-70), and the violence in the lines above of "wild dog" and "flesh" reminds us of the "butcher" of the histories, Richard III, and of the cormorant-villains of the tragedies. The rejection of Falstaff marks the new king's turning from the negligence and excess that had nearly destroyed England since the reign of Richard II. As the young king dismisses one tutor and embraces another in the Chief Justice, he cultivates his garden in "law and form and due proportion":

> The tide of blood in me
> Hath proudly flow'd in vanity till now.
> Now doth it turn and ebb back to the sea,
> Where it shall mingle with the state of floods
> And flow henceforth in formal majesty.
>
> [II:V. ii. 129-133]

The proud river of the private will has become the sea of life of the commonwealth. The blood which here as in the tragedies is the basis of both mood and mind is purged. The man who said he was of all humors comes to achieve the "finely bolted" balance which Henry once thought characterized the traitor Scroop:

> spare in diet,
> Free from gross passion or of mirth or anger . . .
> Not working with the eye without the ear,
> And but in purged judgment trusting neither.
>
> [*H.V.*, II. ii. 131-136]

Henry V is by no means the kind of hero we would admire fully in the tragedies. But the Choruses which celebrate his virtues make perfectly plain that this trim watcher rises from his father's vain engrossing of "cank'red heaps" of gold to genuine magnanimity—the fearless sun king:

> A largess universal, like the sun,
> His liberal eye doth give to every one,
> Thawing cold fear.
>
> [Pro. 4. 43-45]

Falstaff and the Prince

by J. Dover Wilson

. . . *Henry IV*, a play much neglected by both actors and critics, offers to our view the broadest, the most varied, and in some ways the richest champaign in Shakespeare's extensive empire. Much of this, and not the least alluring stretches, must be ignored in what follows, or barely glanced at; Glendower's domain[1] in Part I, for example. . . . The task I have set before me is at once narrow and simple. I am attempting to discover what Professor Charlton has called "the deliberate plan of Shakespeare's play" and, if such a plan existed, how far he succeeded in carrying it into execution.

My title, *The Fortunes of Falstaff*, will suggest the method to be followed. I propose to look for the outlines of Shakespeare's scheme by tracing the career of the knight of Eastcheap. This does not mean that I think him of greater structural consequence than Prince Hal. On the contrary, Falstaff's career is dependent upon Hal's favour, and Hal's favour is determined by that young man's attitude towards his responsibilities as heir to the throne of England. Yet if the Prince's choice spans the play like a great arch, it is Falstaff and his affairs that cover most of the ground.

The title I have selected has, moreover, the convenience of comprising the fortunes, or misfortunes, of the fat rogue outside the pages of Shakespeare. There are, for instance, his pre-natal adventures. He tells

"Falstaff and the Prince." From *The Fortunes of Falstaff* by J. Dover Wilson. (Cambridge: The University Press, 1943), pp. 15-25, 31, 60-70. Reprinted by permission of the Cambridge University Press. The sections reprinted here form parts of two chapters: "The Falstaff Myth" and "The Prince Grows Up." Other parts of those chapters not bearing immediately on the relationship between Falstaff and the Prince have been omitted.

[1] I refer to 3. 1 of Pt. I, which was headed "The Archbishop of Bangor's House in Wales" by Theobald and later editors, though without any warrant in Shakespeare. Glendower behaves like a host throughout the scene, which is clearly a family party.

us that he "was born about three of the clock in the afternoon, with a white head and something of a round belly"; but all the world now knows that he was walking the boards in an earlier, pre-Shakespearian, incarnation, as a comic travesty of Sir John Oldcastle, the famous Lollard leader, who was historically a friend and fellow-soldier of Prince Hal in the reign of Henry IV, but was burnt as a heretic by the same prince when he became King Henry V. He still retained the name Old-castle, as is also well known, in the original version of Shakespeare's play; until the company discovered, or were forcibly reminded, that the wife of the proto-protestant martyr they were guying on the public stage was the revered ancestress of the Cobhams, powerful lords at Elizabeth's court. Worse still, one of these lords was not only of strongly protestant bent, but also, as Lord Chamberlain, actually Shakespeare's official con-troller. Hasty changes in the prompt-book became necessary. How far they extended beyond a mere alteration of names can never be deter-mined, though it seems possible that references to some of Oldcastle's historical or legendary characteristics would require modification. It is even more likely (as Alfred Ainger was, I believe, the first to point out)[2] that traces of Lollardry may still be detected in Falstaff's frequent resort to scriptural phraseology and in his affectation of an uneasy conscience. Of this I shall have something to say later.

First of all, however, I wish to deal with Falstaff's ancestral fortunes of a different kind. As he shares these to a large extent with Prince Hal, a consideration of them should prove helpful in bringing out the main lines of the plot which it is our object to discover.

Riot and the Prodigal Prince

Falstaff may be the most conspicuous, he is certainly the most fascinat-ing, character in *Henry IV*, but all critics are agreed, I believe, that the technical centre of the play is not the fat knight but the lean prince. Hal links the low life with the high life, the scenes at Eastcheap with those at Westminster, the tavern with the battlefield; his doings provide most of the material for both Parts, and with him too lies the future, since he is to become Henry V, the ideal king, in the play that bears his name; finally, the mainspring of the dramatic action is the choice I have already spoken of, the choice he is called upon to make between Vanity and Government, taking the latter in its accepted Tudor meaning, which

[2] *V.* Alfred Ainger, *Lectures and Essays*, 1905, i. pp. 140-55.

includes Chivalry or prowess in the field, the theme of Part I, and Justice, which is the theme of Part II. Shakespeare, moreover, breathes life into these abstractions by embodying them, or aspects of them, in prominent characters, who stand, as it were, about the Prince, like attendant spirits: Falstaff typifying Vanity in every sense of the word, Hotspur Chivalry, of the old anarchic kind, and the Lord Chief Justice the Rule of Law or the new ideal of service to the state.[3]

Thus considered, Shakespeare's *Henry IV* is a Tudor version of a time-honoured theme, already familiar for decades, if not centuries, upon the English stage. Before its final secularization in the first half of the sixteenth century, our drama was concerned with one topic, and one only: human salvation. It was a topic that could be represented in either of two ways: (i) historically, by means of miracle plays, which in the Corpus Christi cycles unrolled before spectators' eyes the whole scheme of salvation from the Creation to the Last Judgement; or (ii) allegorically, by means of morality plays, which exhibited the process of salvation in the individual soul on its road between birth and death, beset with the snares of the World or the wiles of the Evil One. In both kinds the forces of iniquity were allowed full play upon the stage, including a good deal of horse-play, provided they were brought to nought, or safely locked up in Hell, at the end. Salvation remains the supreme interest, however many capers the Devil and his Vice may cut on Everyman's way thither, and always the powers of darkness are withstood, and finally overcome, by the agents of light. But as time went on the religious drama tended to grow longer and more elaborate, after the encyclopaedic fashion of the middle ages, and such development invited its inevitable reaction. With the advent of humanism and the early Tudor court, morality plays became tedious and gave place to lighter and much shorter moral interludes dealing, not with human life as a whole, but with youth and its besetting sins.

An early specimen, entitled *Youth*[4] and composed about 1520, may be taken as typical of the rest. The plot, if plot it can be called, is simplicity itself. The little play opens with a dialogue between Youth and Charity. The young man, heir to his father's land, gives insolent expression to his self-confidence, lustihood, and contempt for spiritual things. Whereupon

---

[3] In what follows I develop a hint in Sir Arthur Quiller-Couch's *Shakespeare's Workmanship*, 1918, p. 148: "The whole of the business [in *Henry IV*] is built on the old Morality structure, imported through the Interlude. Why, it might almost be labelled, after the style of a Morality title, *Contentio inter Virtutem et Vitium de anima Principis*."

[4] *The enterlude of youth*, ed. by W. Bang and R. B. McKerrow, Louvain, 1905.

Charity leaves him, and he is joined by Riot,[5] that is to say wantonness, who presently introduces him to Pride and Lechery. The dialogue then becomes boisterous, and continues in that vein for some time, much no doubt to the enjoyment of the audience. Yet, in the end, Charity reappears with Humility; Youth repents; and the interlude terminates in the most seemly fashion imaginable.

No one, I think, reading this lively playlet, no one certainly who has seen it performed, as I have seen it at the Malvern Festival, can have missed the resemblance between Riot and Falstaff. The words he utters, as he bounces on to the stage at his first entry, gives us the very note of Falstaff's gaiety:

> Huffa! huffa! who calleth after me?
> I am Riot full of jollity.
> My heart is as light as the wind,
> And all on riot is my mind,
> Wheresoever I go.

And the parallel is even more striking in other respects. Riot, like Falstaff, escapes from tight corners with a quick dexterity; like Falstaff, commits robbery on the highway; like Falstaff, jests immediately afterwards with his young friend on the subject of hanging; and like Falstaff, invites him to spend the stolen money at a tavern, where, he promises, "We will drink diuers wine" and "Thou shalt haue a wench to kysse Whansoeuer thou wilte"; allurements which prefigure the Boar's Head and Mistress Doll Tearsheet.

But Youth at the door of opportunity, with Age or Experience, Charity or Good Counsel, offering him the yoke of responsibility, while the World, the Flesh, and the Devil beckon him to follow them on the primrose way to the everlasting bonfire, is older than even the medieval religious play. It is a theme to which every generation gives fresh form, while retaining its eternal substance. Young men are the heroes of the Plautine and Terentian comedy which delighted the Roman world; and these young men, generally under the direction of a clever slave or parasite, disport themselves, and often hoodwink their old fathers, for most of the play, until they too settle down in the end. The same theme appears in a very different story, the parable of the Prodigal Son. And the similarity of the two struck humanist teachers of the early sixteenth century with

---

[5] riot = "wanton, loose, or wasteful living; debauchery, dissipation, extravagance" (*O.E.D.*). Cf. the Prodigal Son, who "wasted his substance with riotous living" (Luke xv. 13).

such force that, finding Terence insufficiently edifying for their pupils to act, they developed a "Christian Terence" by turning the parable into Latin plays, of which many examples by different authors have come down to us.[6] In these plot and structure are much the same. The opening scene shows us Acolastus, the prodigal, demanding his portion, receiving good counsel from his father, and going off into a far country. Then follow three or four acts of entertainment almost purely Terentian in atmosphere, in which he wastes his substance in riotous living and falls at length to feeding with the pigs. Finally, in the last act he returns home, penniless and repentant, to receive his pardon. This ingenious blend of classical comedy and humanistic morality preserves, it will be noted, the traditional ratio between edification and amusement, and distributes them in the traditional manner. So long as the serious note is duly emphasized at the beginning and end of the play, almost any quantity of fun, often of the most unseemly nature, was allowed and expected during the intervening scenes.

All this, and much more of a like character, gave the pattern for Shakespeare's *Henry IV*. Hal associates Falstaff in turn with the Devil of the miracle play, the Vice of the morality, and the Riot of the interlude, when he calls him "that villainous abominable misleader of Youth, that old white-bearded Satan," [7] "that reverend Vice, that grey Iniquity, that father Ruffian, that Vanity in years," [8] and "the tutor and the feeder of my riots," [9] "Riot," again, is the word that comes most readily to King Henry's lips when speaking of his prodigal son's misconduct.[10] And, as heir to the Vice, Falstaff inherits by reversion the functions and attributes of the Lord of Misrule, the Fool, the Buffoon, and the Jester, antic figures the origins of which are lost in the dark backward and abysm of folk-custom.[11] We shall find that Falstaff possesses a strain, and more

---

[6] V. C. H. Herford, *The Literary Relations between England and Germany in the Sixteenth Century*, 1886, ch. III, pp. 84-95.

[7] Pt. I, 2. 4. 450 (508); cf. l. 435 (491): "Thou art violently carried away from grace, there is a devil haunts thee in the likeness of an old fat man."

[8] *Ibid.* 2. 4. 442 (500).   [9] Pt. II, 5. 5. 63 (66).

[10] Cf. Pt. I, 1. 1. 85: "Riot and dishonour stain the brow/Of my young Harry"; Pt. II, 4. 4. 62: "His headstrong riot hath no curb," 4. 5. 135: "When that my care could not withhold thy riots,/What wilt thou do when riot is thy care?"

[11] In particular, the exact significance of the Vice is exasperatingly obscure. Cf. the discussion by Sir E. K. Chambers (*Medieval Stage*, ii, pp. 203-5), who concludes "that whatever the name may mean . . . the character of the vice is derived from that of the domestic fool or jester." I hazard the suggestion that it was originally the title or name of the Fool who attended upon the Lord of Misrule; *v.* Feuillerat, *Revels of the time of Edward VI*, p. 73: "One vyces dagger & a ladle with a bable pendante . . . deliuerid to the Lorde of Mysrules foole."

than a strain, of the classical *miles gloriosus* as well. In short, the Falstaff-Hal plot embodies a composite myth which had been centuries amaking, and was for the Elizabethans full of meaning that has largely disappeared since then: which is one reason why we have come so seriously to misunderstand the play.

Nor was Shakespeare the first to see Hal as the prodigal. The legend of Harry of Monmouth began to grow soon after his death in 1422; and practically all the chroniclers, even those writing in the fifteenth century, agree on his wildness in youth and on the sudden change that came upon him at his accession to the throne. The essence of Shakespeare's plot is, indeed, already to be found in the following passage about King Henry V taken from Fabyan's *Chronicle* of 1516:

> This man, before the death of his fader, applyed him unto all vyce and insolency, and drewe unto hym all ryottours and wylde disposed persones; but after he was admytted to the rule of the lande, anone and suddenly he became a newe man, and tourned al that rage into sobernesse and wyse sadness, and the vyce into constant vertue. And for he wolde contynewe the vertue, and not to be reduced thereunto by the familiarytie of his olde nyse company, he therefore, after rewardes to them gyuen, charged theym upon payne of theyr lyues, that none of theym were so hardy to come within x. myle of such place as he were lodgyd, after a day by him assigned.[12]

There appears to be no historical basis for any of this, and Kingsford has plausibly suggested that its origin may be "contemporary scandal which attached to Henry through his youthful association with the unpopular Lollard leader" Sir John Oldcastle. "It is noteworthy," he points out, "that Henry's political opponents were Oldcastle's religious persecutors; and also that those writers who charge Henry with wildness as Prince find his peculiar merit as King in the maintaining of Holy Church and destroying of heretics. A supposed change in his attitude on questions of religion may possibly furnish a partial solution for his alleged 'change suddenly into a new man.' "[13] The theory is the more attractive that it would account not only for Hal's conversion but also for Oldcastle's degradation from a protestant martyr and distinguished soldier to what Ainger calls "a broken-down Lollard, a fat old sensualist, retaining just sufficient recollection of the studies of his more serious days to be able to point his jokes with them."

Yet when all is said, the main truth seems to be that the fifteenth and

[12] Fabyan's *Chronicle*, 1516, p. 577.
[13] C. L. Kingsford, *The First English Life of King Henry the Fifth*, 1911, pp. xlii, xliii.

early sixteenth centuries, the age of allegory in poetry and morality in drama, needed a Prodigal Prince, whose miraculous conversion might be held up as an example by those concerned (as what contemporary political writer was not?) with the education of young noblemen and princes. And could any more alluring fruits of repentance be offered such pupils than the prowess and statesmanship of Henry V, the hero of Agincourt, the mirror of English kingship for a hundred years? In his miracle play, *Richard II*, Shakespeare had celebrated the traditional royal martyr;[14] in his morality play, *Henry IV*, he does the like with the traditional royal prodigal.

He made the myth his own, much as musicians adopt and absorb a folk-tune as the theme for a symphony. He glorified it, elaborated it, translated it into what were for the Elizabethans modern terms, and exalted it into a heaven of delirious fun and frolic; yet never, for a moment, did he twist it from its original purpose, which was serious, moral, didactic. Shakespeare plays no tricks with his public. He did not, like Euripides, dramatize the stories of his race and religion in order to subvert the traditional ideals those stories were first framed to set forth. Prince Hal is the prodigal, and his repentance is not only to be taken seriously, it is to be admired and commended. Moreover, the story of the prodigal, secularized and modernized as it might be, ran the same course as ever and contained the same three principal characters: the tempter, the younker, and the father with property to bequeath and counsel to give. It followed also the fashion set by miracle, morality and the Christian Terence by devoting much attention to the doings of the first-named. Shakespeare's audience enjoyed the fascination of Prince Hal's "white-bearded Satan" for two whole plays, as perhaps no character on the world's stage had ever been enjoyed before. But they knew, from the beginning, that the reign of this marvellous Lord of Misrule must have an end, that Falstaff must be rejected by the Prodigal Prince, when the time for reformation came. And they no more thought of questioning or disapproving of that finale, than their ancestors would have thought of protesting against the Vice being carried off to Hell at the end of the interlude.

The main theme, therefore, of Shakespeare's morality play is the growing-up of a madcap prince into the ideal king, who was Henry V; and the play was made primarily—already made by some dramatist before Shakespeare took it over—in order to exhibit his conversion and to reveal his character unfolding towards that end, as he finds himself

---

[14] *V.* pp. xvi-xix, lviii-lix of my Introd. to *Richard II,* 1939 ("The New Shakespeare").

faced more and more directly by his responsibilities. It is that which determines its very shape. Even the "fearful symmetry" of Falstaff's own person was welded upon the anvil of that purpose. It is probably because the historical Harry of Monmouth "exceded the meane stature of men," as his earliest chronicler tells us; "his necke . . . longe, his body slender and leane, his boanes smale," [15]—because in Falstaff's words he actually was a starveling, an eel-skin, a tailor's yard, and all the rest of it —that the idea of Falstaff himself as "a huge hill of flesh" first came to Shakespeare.[16] It was certainly, at any rate in part, in order to explain and palliate the Prince's love of rioting and wantonness that he set out to make Falstaff as enchanting as he could.[17] And he succeeded so well that the young man now lies under the stigma, not of having yielded to the tempter, but of disentangling himself, in the end, from his toils. After all, Falstaff *is* "a devil . . . in the likeness of an old fat man," and the Devil has generally been supposed to exercise limitless attraction in his dealings with the sons of men. A very different kind of poet, who imagined a very different kind of Satan, has been equally and similarly misunderstood by modern critics, who no longer believing in the Prince of Darkness have ceased to understand him. For, as Professor R. W. Chambers reminded us in his last public utterance,[18] when Blake declared that Milton was "of the Devil's party without knowing it," he overlooked the fact, and his many successors have likewise overlooked the fact, that, if the fight in Heaven, the struggle in Eden, the defeat of Adam and Eve, and the victory of the Second Adam in *Paradise Regained,* are to appear in their true proportions, we must be made to realize how

[15] Kingsford, *op. cit.* p. 16.

[16] Ainger tries to persuade himself that there was a tradition associating the Lollard, Oldcastle, with extreme fatness; but his editor, Beeching, is obliged to admit in a footnote that he is not aware of any references to this fatness before Shakespeare; *v.* Ainger, *op. cit.* pp. 126-30.

[17] Cf. H. N. Hudson, *Shakespeare: his Life, Art and Characters* (ed. 1888), ii, p. 83: "It must be no ordinary companionship that yields entertainment to such a spirit [as Prince Hal's] even in his loosest moments. Whatever bad or questionable elements may mingle with his mirth, it must have some fresh and rich ingredients, some sparkling and generous flavour, to make him relish it. Anything like vulgar rowdyism cannot fail of disgusting him. His ears were never organised to that sort of music. Here then we have a sort of dramatic necessity for the character of Falstaff. To answer the purpose it was imperative that he should be just such a marvellous congregation of charms and vices as he is." See also A. H. Tolman, *Falstaff and other Shakespearian Topics,* 1925, and W. W. Lawrence, *Shakespeare's Problem Comedies,* 1931, p. 64 (an interesting contrast between Hal and Falstaff, Bertram and Parolles).

[18] *Poets and their Critics: Langland and Milton* (British Academy Warton Lecture), 1941, pp. 29-30.

immeasurable, how indomitable, is the spirit of the Great Enemy. It may also be noted that Milton's Son of God has in modern times been charged with priggishness no less freely than Shakespeare's son of Bolingbroke.

Shakespeare, I say, translated his myth into a language and endued it with an atmosphere that his contemporaries would best appreciate. First, Hal is not only youth or the prodigal, he is the young prodigal *prince,* the youthful heir to the throne. The translation, then, already made by the chroniclers, if Kingsford be right, from sectarian terms into those more broadly religious or moral, now takes us out of the theological into the political sphere. This is seen most clearly in the discussion of the young king's remarkable conversion by the two bishops at the beginning of *Henry V.* King Henry, as Bradley notes, "is much more obviously religious than most of Shakespeare's heroes," [19] so that one would expect the bishops to interpret his change of life as a religious conversion. Yet they say nothing about religion except that he is "a true lover of the holy church" and can "reason in divinity"; the rest of their talk, some seventy lines, is concerned with learning and statecraft. In fact, the conversation of these worldly prelates demonstrates that the conversion is not the old repentance for sin and amendment of life, which is the burden, as we have seen, of Fabyan and other chroniclers, but a repentance of the renaissance type, which transforms an idle and wayward prince into an excellent soldier and governor. Even King Henry IV, at the bitterest moments of the scenes with his son, never taxes him with sin, and his only use of the word refers to sins that would multiply in the country, when

> the fifth Harry from curbed licence plucks
> The muzzle of restraint.[20]

If Hal had sinned, it was not against God, but against Chivalry, against Justice, against his father, against the interests of the crown, which was the keystone of England's political and social stability. Instead of educating himself for the burden of kingship, he had been frittering away his time, and making himself cheap, with low companions

> that daff the world aside
> And bid it pass.

In a word, a word that Shakespeare applies no less than six times to his conduct, he is guilty of Vanity. And Vanity, though not in the theological

[19] *Oxford Lectures*, p. 256.
[20] Pt. II, 4. 5. 131.

category of the Seven Deadly Sins, was a cardinal iniquity in a young prince or nobleman of the sixteenth and seventeenth centuries; almost as heinous, in fact, as Idleness in an apprentice. I am not suggesting that this represents Shakespeare's own view. Of Shakespeare's views upon the problems of conduct, whether in prince or commoner, we are in general ignorant, though he seems to hint in both *Henry IV* and *Henry V* that the Prince of Wales learnt some lessons at least from Falstaff and his crew, Francis and his fellow-drawers, which stood him in good stead when he came to rule the country and command troops in the field. But it is the view that his father and his own conscience take of his mistreadings; and, as the spectators would take it as well, we must regard it as the thesis to which Shakespeare addressed himself.

When, however, he took audiences by storm in 1597 and 1598 with his double *Henry IV* he gave them something much more than a couple of semi-mythical figures from the early fifteenth century, brought up to date politically. He presented persons and situations at once fresh and actual. Both Hal and Falstaff are denizens of Elizabethan London. Hal thinks, acts, comports himself as an heir to the Queen might have done, had she delighted her people by taking a consort and giving them a Prince of Wales; while Falstaff symbolizes, on the one hand, all the feasting and good cheer for which Eastcheap stood, and reflects, on the other, the shifts, subterfuges, and shady tricks that decayed gentlemen and soldiers were put to if they wished to keep afloat and gratify their appetites in the London underworld of the late sixteenth century.

* * *

The prodigiously incarnate Riot, who fills the Boar's Head with his jollity, typifies much more, of course, than the pleasures of the table. He stands for a whole globe of happy continents, and his laughter is "broad as ten thousand beeves at pasture." [21] But he is Feasting first, and his creator never allows us to forget it. For in this way he not only perpetually associates him in our minds with appetizing images, but contrives that as we laugh at his wit our souls shall be satisfied as with marrow and fatness. No one has given finer expression to this satisfaction than Hazlitt, and I may fitly round off the topic with words of his:

> Falstaff's wit is an emanation of a fine constitution; an exuberance of
> good-humour and good-nature; an overflowing of his love of laughter and
> good-fellowship; a giving vent to his heart's ease, and over-contentment with

[21] George Meredith, *The Spirit of Shakespeare.*

himself and others. He would not be in character, if he were not so fat as he is; for there is the greatest keeping in the boundless luxury of his imagination and the pampered self-indulgence of his physical appetites. He manures and nourishes his mind with jests, as he does his body with sack and sugar. He carves out his jokes, as he would a capon or a haunch of venison, where there is *cut and come again;* and pours out upon them the oil of gladness. His tongue drops fatness, and in the chambers of his brain "it snows of meat and drink." He keeps perpetually holiday and open house, and we live with him in a round of invitations to a rump and dozen. . . . He never fails to enrich his discourse with allusions to eating and drinking, but we never see him at table. He carries his own larder about with him, and is himself "a tun of man." [22]

*   *   *

The Truant's Return to Chivalry

In *Henry IV* Shakespeare handles, among other human relationships, the disharmony that often arises between parent and child as the latter begins to grow up. It is a difficult time in any walk of life; but strained relations between a reigning sovereign, of either sex, and the heir to the throne seem almost to partake of the order of nature. Within living memory there have been two examples at Windsor, while the story of Wilhelm II of Germany and his mother shows that it is not necessarily a product of the English climate. Individual instances are, of course, attended by special circumstances, and the attitude of Henry IV towards his son was to some extent the result of the peculiar conditions of his own accession. He had usurped the throne from Richard II, whom he subsequently murdered; he was not even Richard's heir, Mortimer his cousin being next in lineal succession. Thus his reign and all his actions are overhung with the consciousness both of personal guilt and of insecurity of tenure, a fact that Shakespeare never misses an opportunity of underlining. "Uneasy lies the head that usurps a crown" might be taken as the motto of what Johnson calls the "tragical part" of the play, and the worry of it, combined with ill-health, finally wears the King out. As one of his sons says,

> Th'incessant care and labour of his mind
> Hath wrought the mure that should confine it in
> So thin that life looks through and will break out.[23]

[22] *Characters of Shakespeare's Plays* (Hazlitt's *Works,* ed. A. R. Waller and A. Glover, 1902, i. 278).
[23] Pt. II, 4. 4. 118-20.

Whatever Bolingbroke may be in *Richard II,* King Henry IV is no hard
crafty politician but a man sick in body and spirit, a pathetic figure.
In the hope of purging his soul of the crimes that gained him his throne,
he dreams of a crusade; and Heaven's anger at those crimes seems to
him most evident in the strange, disastrous behaviour of his heir. He
misunderstands his son, of course, misunderstands him completely; but
it is the nature of fathers to misunderstand their sons.

As for the son himself, Princes of Wales have so often in youth chosen
to break away from court formalities and live at freedom—with boon
companions of their own choosing, that we might take Prince Hal's situation as the almost inevitable consequence of his position in life. There
are special points, however, about his situation too which should not be
overlooked. At the opening of the play, for instance, the quarrel had
been going on for some time. He speaks, at the first interview with his
father, of

> The long grown wounds of my intemperature;[24]

and at least twelve months before, at the end of *Richard II,* we have
Bolingbroke referring to the wild courses of his "young, wanton and
effeminate boy." Hal is historically little more than sixteen years old at
the battle of Shrewsbury, and though he seems twenty at least in Shakespeare, he must have been very young when first, under the guidance of
Poins we may surmise, he became "an Ephesian of the old church" and
got to know Falstaff at the Boar's Head; a point to be borne in mind
in our judgement of him. His conduct, again, has not only brought him
into public contempt, as is proved by Hotspur's references in the third
scene, but has led to the loss of his seat at the Privy Council and his banishment from the court, as the King informs us at the first interview.[25]
Thus the breach between father and son is not only of long standing but
has gone deep. On the other hand, we learn from the Prince's soliloquy
already dealt with that he is now tiring of his unchartered freedom, and
looking forward vaguely to the day when he will resume the responsibilities of his station. In a word, he is ceasing to be a boy. As the play
goes forward, we are in fact to watch him growing up and becoming a
man, and a man, do not let us forget, who represents the ideal king,
whether leader or governor, in Elizabethan eyes.

One more point, a technical point, should be brought out in this connection. Critics complain that Hal's character is "not the offspring of

[24] Pt. I, 3. 2. 156.
[25] *Ibid.* 3. 2. 32-5.

the poet's reflection and passion." [26] Does this amount to anything more than a statement that he is not so self-revealing as Hamlet, or Macbeth or Richard II or even Harry Hotspur? The kind of reserve that springs from absence of self-regard is, in point of fact, one of his principal characteristics; and such a feature is difficult to represent in dialogue. Everything depends upon bearing, expression of countenance, silences, just those things which can hardly, if at all, be conveyed in a book. All that remains of Shakespeare is his book; his directions to the players are gone beyond recall. We have, therefore, no means of telling just how he wished Hal to be played. But we have equally no right to assume that Hal is heartless, because he does not, like Richard II, wear his heart upon his sleeve. He is just not interested in Hal and so does not talk about him, except banteringly in the Falstaff scenes. And there is more than natural reserve to be reckoned with. By the very nature of his material Shakespeare was restricted in his opportunities of exhibiting the Prince's character. While he is in disgrace, and his creator is obliged to keep him more or less thus eclipsed until the death of his father, Hal can only be shown in speech with his boon companions, and in an occasional interview with the King. Why not, it may be said, give him his Horatio like Hamlet? The answer is that Shakespeare does so; he gives him Poins, and the discovery of the worthlessness of this friend is the subject of one of the most moving and revealing scenes in which the Prince figures.[27] In view of all this, to assert, as Bradley does, that Hal is incapable of tenderness or affection except towards members of his own family,[28] is surely a quite unwarranted assumption. We shall find it directly contradicted by dramatic facts which emerge at a later stage. For the present we have to rest content with what we may glean from the talk he has with his father, but we need feel under no necessity of discounting what he then says and does as prompted solely by family ties or dynastic policy.

The insurrection of the Percies obliges the King to summon the Prince of Wales, that he may find out exactly where he stands and if he can be made use of in this crisis which threatens the newly established dynasty; and we are prepared for an interview, by Sir John Bracy's summons, which interrupts the jollification at the Boar's Head, and by Falstaff and Hal themselves, who rehearse the scene in comic anticipation.[29] His

[26] Peter Alexander, *Shakespeare's Life and Art,* 1938, p. 120.

[27] Pt. II, 2. 2.

[28] *Oxford Lectures,* p. 258.

[29] Such anticipation follows, it should be noted, the time-honoured practice of the old religious plays; cf. the comic scene of *The Second Shepherd's Play,* in which the shepherds present their gifts to Mak's wife and the supposed child, which immediately precedes that in which offerings are made to the Holy Child.

Majesty begins with bitter chiding, as Falstaff had prophesied he would. He hints at the affair with the Lord Chief Justice (to which Shakespeare makes no direct reference before Part II), and speaks of the lost seat at the Council and the banishment from court. But the burden of his charge is that Harry has made himself cheap in the eyes of men, which is the very last thing the representative of a family with a doubtful title to the throne should permit himself. He compares him with the reckless, feckless, Richard II—Henry can never stop thinking about Richard—who had also come to grief through making himself cheap, while he likens Hotspur, stealing away men's hearts by prowess and policy, to himself before he pushed Richard from his stool. Finally he turns upon his son, calls him his "nearest, dearest enemy," and concludes with an outburst declaring him

> like enough through vassal fear,
> Base inclination and the start of spleen,
> To fight against me under Percy's pay.

From beginning to end of the interview the Prince's attitude is perfect, as it ever is with his father. He accepts the blame as in part deserved, though protesting that his scrapes have been grossly exaggerated by "smiling pickthanks and base newsmongers." He promises with a noble and touching simplicity, in which dignity mingles with humility,

> I shall hereafter, my thrice gracious lord,
> Be more myself.

But the King's last bitter taunt stings him in self-defence to proclaim more positive intentions; he will reinstate himself in the eyes of his father (it is characteristic that he speaks and thinks of no rehabilitation of a more public kind) by meeting Hotspur on the battlefield and wresting the crown of chivalry from his brow. The King, convinced by the fervour of the protest, restores him to his favour and confidence, and even associates him in the command of the army of the west. Thus the feet of the Prince are definitely set upon the path of reformation. The rebellion has brought him an earlier opportunity than he hoped of

> breaking through the foul and ugly mists
> Of vapours that did seem to strangle him.

Yet the process is not to be carried out in a day. It is, in fact, a double

process, comprising two distinct stages. As a "truant to chivalry" [30] he
has first to prove himself a soldier and a leader; and this he accomplishes
on the field of Shrewsbury. It is only later that the companion of Riot
has a chance of displaying the qualities, or acknowledging the loyalties,
of the governor. Viewing *Henry IV* as a whole, we may label Part I the
Return to Chivalry; Part II the Atonement with Justice.

Shakespeare cannot bring horsemen upon the stage, but he depicts
his young knight for us in the words of Sir Richard Vernon, who bears
news to the rebel camp of the approach of the King's forces towards
Shrewsbury. "Where" Hotspur contemptuously asks him,

> Where is his son,
> The nimble-footed madcap Prince of Wales,
> And his comrades, that daff the world aside,
> And bid it pass?

To which Vernon replies:

> All furnished, all in arms;
> All plumed like estridges that wing the wind,
> Baited like eagles having lately bathed,
> Glittering in golden coats like images,
> As full of spirit as the month of May,
> And gorgeous as the sun at midsummer;
> Wanton as youthful goats, wild as young bulls.
> I saw young Harry with his beaver on,
> His cuisses on his thighs, gallantly armed,
> Rise from the ground like feathered Mercury,
> And vaulted with such ease into his seat,
> As if an angel dropped down from the clouds,
> To turn and wind a fiery Pegasus,
> And witch the world with noble horsemanship.[31]

"A more lively representation," comments Dr. Johnson, "of young men
ardent for enterprize, perhaps no writer has ever given." And that Shakespeare in penning these lines, turned for inspiration to Spenser's description of the Red Cross Knight rising lusty as an eagle from the Well of
Life shows (i) that he desired to call up a vision of chivalry in its perfec-

---

[30] Pt. I, 5. 1. 94.   [31] Pt. I, 4. 1. 94-110.

tion, and (ii) that in evoking this vision he had specially in mind the notion of regeneration.

It is Vernon again who tells us that the Prince has a knightly bearing and action in keeping with his appearance as a warrior. Speaking of the challenge which he and Worcester are commissioned by the Prince to convey to Hotspur, he declares:

> I never in my life
> Did hear a challenge urged more modestly,
> Unless a brother should a brother dare
> To gentle exercise and proof of arms.[32]

And he goes on to stress, in glowing terms, a generosity of spirit towards his rival and a humble-mindedness when speaking of himself, which reminds us, on the one hand, of Hamlet's courtesy to Laertes before the duel and, on the other, of the attitude of Malory's Lancelot towards his fellow-knights.

In the battle scenes themselves, Shakespeare bends all his energy to enhance the honour of his hero, even departing from the chroniclers to do so. The conspicuous part he plays is exhibited in marked contrast to that of the King. The King, for example, dresses many men in his coats so as to shield himself: the wounded Hal refuses to withdraw to his tent, yet is all the while glowing with pride at his younger brother's prowess. Holinshed, again, says nothing of the Prince coming to his father's rescue, when sore beset by the terrible Douglas; but Shakespeare borrows this significant detail from the poet Daniel and elaborates it. Indeed, throughout the battle we are made to feel that the Prince is the real leader and inspirer of the royal army, a role which Holinshed ascribes to the King. There follows the encounter and fight with Hotspur, also taken from Daniel, which would be realistically played on the Elizabethan stage, and the tender, almost brotherly, speech which he utters over his slain foe. This last is Shakespeare's alone. Furthermore, Shakespeare gives the gentle victor an action to match his words worthy of the occasion in a supreme degree; an action the recovery of which I owe to an American scholar.[33]

> But let my favours hide thy mangled face,

says the Prince bending forward to cover those staring eyes,

---

[32] *Ibid.* 5. 2. 53 ff.
[33] See the article by H. Hartman, *Pub. Mod. Lang. Assoc.* 1931.

> And even in thy behalf I'll thank myself
> For doing these fair rites of tenderness.[34]

The thought, all the more charming for its boyishness, is prompted by a rush of generous emotion. But what are these favours, these rites of tenderness? The fight over, the Prince has removed his beaver and holds it in his hand. The "favours" it bears are Prince of Wales's feathers, one or two of which he now reverently lays across the face of his mighty enemy. It is a gesture worthy of Sir Philip Sidney himself; the crowning touch in the vision Shakespeare gives us of his paladin Prince, brave as a lion, tender as a woman.

As he turns from the body of Hotspur, Hal sees a vaster corpse nearby, and is moved to utter another epitaph in a different key.

> What! old acquaintance! could not all this flesh
> Keep in a little life? poor Jack, farewell!
> I could have better spared a better man:
> O, I should have a heavy miss of thee,
> If I were much in love with vanity!

There is genuine sorrow here; Falstaff had given him too much pleasure and amusement for him to face his death without a pang. But the tone, which may be compared with Hamlet's when confronted with Yorick's skull, is that of a prince speaking of his dead jester, not of friend taking leave of familiar friend; and what there is of affection is mainly retrospective. In the new world that opens up at Shrewsbury there is little place left for the follies of the past.

> O, I should have a heavy miss of thee,
> If I were much in love with vanity.

It is Hal's real farewell to the old life; and after Shrewsbury Falstaff is never again on the same terms with his patron.

The two epitaphs are deliberately placed side by side. Can there be any reasonable doubt which seemed to Shakespeare the more important? The overthrow of Hotspur is the turning point not only of the political plot of the two Parts but also in the development of the Prince's character. The son has fulfilled the promises made to his father; the heir has freed

---

[34] Pt. I, 5. 4. 96 ff.

the monarchy of its deadliest foe; the youth has proved, to himself, that he need fear no rival in Britain as soldier and general. Yet these are not the considerations first in his mind; for himself and his own affairs are never uppermost in the consciousness of this character. The epitaph on Hotspur contains not a word of triumph; its theme is the greatness of the slain man's spirit, the tragedy of his fall, and what may be done to reverence him in death. With such solemn thoughts does Shakespeare's hero turn to Falstaff. Is it surprising that he should be out of love with Vanity at a moment like this? The point is of interest technically, since the moment balances and adumbrates a still more solemn moment at the end of Part II in which he also encounters Falstaff and has by then come to be even less in love with what he represents.

How little the sense of personal triumph enters into what he feels about the overthrow of Hotspur is shown by his willingness to surrender all claims when his "old acquaintance" surprisingly comes to life again and asserts that the honour belongs to him.

> For my part, if a lie may do thee grace,
> I'll gild it with the happiest terms I have,

is his good-humoured aside. It is in keeping with the easy amiability which first took him to the Boar's Head and made him popular with the drawers when he got there. But it is also an instance of selflessness and generosity which appears to have been as much overlooked by critics as have its effects upon the character of Falstaff in Part II.[35] For the Prince keeps his promise, and it will be noticed that the King shows no consciousness in the next scene of Part I, which is the last, that his son has had any share in the slaying of his chief enemy.

All that Shakespeare does for the Prince in this scene, which might so easily have been converted into one of public triumph and applause on his behalf, is to offer yet another example of his native magnanimity. Douglas, a captured fugitive, lies bruised at his tent and in his power. He desires the King to grant him the disposal of this great soldier; and when consent is given he turns to the brother who had just fleshed his maiden sword and bids him deliver the captive

> Up to his pleasure, ransomless and free,

inasmuch as

---

[35] H. N. Hudson, as usual, is the only critic to see the facts; cf. *infra*, ch. v, 32 note.

His valour shown upon our crests to-day
Hath taught us how to cherish such high deeds,
Even in the bosom of our adversaries.

The "high courtesy"of this act, which would seem of the very essence of chivalry to Elizabethans and can still win our admiration in an age of tanks and bombs, could only have occurred to a spirit of real nobility. That the same spirit should then bestow upon another the delight of its execution more than doubles the quality of its gallantry. Sir Lancelot himself could not have been more courteous, more self-effacing.

Shakespeare inherited from chroniclers a sudden conversion for Prince Hal of an almost miraculous kind. This he is at pains to make reasonable and human, and he does so by marking it off, as I have said, into various stages, thereby accustoming the audience more and more to the notion of it and giving an impression of gradual development of character, the development of a kind normal in the passage from adolescence to manhood. There is so much else to be done in the play, that he cannot, as in *Hamlet,* keep the young man constantly beneath the limelight of our attention; he has scope for intermittent glimpses only. But these glimpses are given us at the right moments, and are fully sufficient for the purpose, if we are following the play with the attention a dramatist may legitimately expect; an expectation thwarted unfortunately in the present instance by the fact that the play is never seen as a whole upon the modern stage and that the intense preoccupation of the romantic critics with the character of Falstaff has thrown a shadow of obscurity over all the scenes and characters in which he is not directly concerned. In Part I we are afforded three opportunities of seeing the mind of the Prince, in each of which he appears more conscious than before of the obligations of his vocation: (i) the soliloquy after his first scene with Falstaff in which he is shown growing tired of tavern life and trying, in a rather boyish fashion, to palliate, as Johnson says, "those follies which he can neither justify nor forsake"; (ii) the interview with his father, in which, awakened for the first time to the full significance of his position by the appalling suspicions of disloyalty which the King entertains, he takes a solemn vow to meet Hotspur in the field and either rob him of his title as the flower of chivalry or perish in the attempt; and (iii) the battle of Shrewsbury, the climax of Part I, in which for some six scenes he is brought continuously before us, either in person or through the report of other characters, so that we see more of him than we have ever seen before, and discover him to be not only a general who can win a battle and a soldier who can beat to the ground the best swordsman in the country, not only the soul of courtesy, whose chief thought is respect for the defeated and tenderness for the fallen, but a man so large-hearted and unmindful of self that, having wrested the laurels of the age from Hotspur's brow, he loses interest in the garland itself, is only amused when Falstaff, finding it lying in his way, sets it on his own head, and promises to aid and abet the fraud, as a favour to a friend and a jest to himself.

Introduction to *Henry V*

by J. H. Walter

The Epic Nature of the Play and Its Implications—the Ideal King

Poor Henry! the chorus of critics sings both high and low, now as low as "Mars, his idiot," now as high as "This star of England." It is strangely ironical that a play in which the virtue of unity is so held up for imitation should provoke so much disunity among its commentators. More recently Tillyard, *Shakespeare's History Plays,* 1944, and Dover Wilson have examined the play from fresh aspects. Tillyard considers that the weight of historical and legendary tradition hampered Shakespeare too greatly; that the inconsistencies of Henry's miraculously changed character, the picture of the ideal king and the good mixer were "impossible of worthy fulfilment." Dover Wilson praises Shakespeare's attempt to deal with the epic form of the story, and he writes with justice and with moving eloquence on the heroic spirit that informs the play. Both pose important questions without following up the implications of their own terms. It is necessary, therefore, to make some general observations on the relationship of *Henry V* to epic poetry, to the ideal king and, very briefly, to the view of history in the intellectual fashions of the day.

The reign of Henry V was fit matter for an epic. Daniel omits apologetically Henry's reign from his *Civil Wars,* but pauses to comment,

> O what eternal matter here is found
> Whence new immortal *Iliads* might proceed;

and there is little doubt that this was also the opinion of his contemporaries, for not only was its theme of proper magnitude, but it also agreed

"Introduction to *Henry V*." From *King Henry V,* ed. J. H. Walter, *The Arden Edition of the Works of William Shakespeare* (London: Methuen and Co. Ltd., 1954), pp. xiv-xxxii. Reprinted by permission of Methuen and Co. Ltd. Sections 3, 4, and 5 of Walter's "Introduction" are reproduced here.

with Aristotle's pronouncement that the epic fable should be matter of history. Shakespeare, therefore, in giving dramatic form to material of an epic nature was faced with difficulties. Not the least was noted by Jonson, following Aristotle, "As to a *Tragedy* or a Comedy, the Action may be convenient, and perfect, that would not fit an *Epicke Poeme* in Magnitude" (*Discoveries,* ed. 1933, p. 102). Again, while Shakespeare took liberties with the unity of action in his plays, insistence on unity of action was also a principle of epic construction (*Discoveries,* p. 105) and could not lightly be ignored. Finally, the purpose of epic poetry was the moral one of arousing admiration and encouraging imitation. Sidney writes,

> as the image of each action styrreth and instructeth the mind, so the loftie image of such Worthies most inflameth the mind with desire to be worthy, and informes with counsel how to be worthy (*Apologie,* p. 33).

Shakespeare's task was not merely to extract material for a play from an epic story, but within the physical limits of the stage and within the admittedly inadequate dramatic convention to give the illusion of an epic whole. In consequence *Henry V* is daringly novel, nothing quite like it had been seen on the stage before. No wonder Shakespeare, after the magnificent epic invocation of the Prologue, becomes apologetic; no wonder he appeals most urgently to his audiences to use their imagination, for in daring to simulate the "best and most accomplished kinde of Poetry" (*Apologie,* p. 33) on the common stage he laid himself open to the scorn and censure of the learned and judicious.

Dover Wilson points out that Shakespeare accepted the challenge of the epic form by writing a series of historic tableaux and emphasizing the epical tone "by a Chorus, who speaks five prologues and an epilogue." Undoubtedly the speeches of the Chorus are epical in tone, but they have another epical function, for in the careful way they recount the omitted details of the well-known story, they secure unity of action. Shakespeare, in fact, accepts Sidney's advice to follow the ancient writers of tragedy and "by some *Nuncius* to recount thinges done in former time or other place" (*Apologie,* p. 53). Indeed, it is possible that the insistent emphasis on action in unity in I. ii. 180-213, with illustrations drawn from music, bees, archery, sundials, the confluence of roads and streams, is, apart from its immediate context, a reflection of Shakespeare's concern with unity of action in the structure of the play.

The moral values of the epic will to a large extent depend on the character and action of the epic hero, who in renaissance theory must be perfect above the common run of men and of royal blood, in effect, the ideal king. Now the ideal king was a very real conception. From Isocrates onwards attempts had been made to compile the virtues essential to such a ruler. Christian writers had made free use of classical works until the idea reached its most influential form in the *Institutio Principis*, 1516, of Erasmus. Elyot and other sixteenth century writers borrowed from Erasmus; indeed, there is so much repetition and rearranging of the same material that it is impossible to be certain of the dependence of one writer upon another. Shakespeare knew Elyot's *Governor,* yet he seems closer in his general views to the *Institutio* and to Chelidonius' treatise translated from Latin into French by Bouvaisteau and from French into English by Chillester as *Of the Institution and firste beginning of Christian Princes,* 1571. How much Shakespeare had assimilated these ideas will be obvious from the following collection of parallels from Erasmus,[1] Chelidonius and *Henry V.*

It is assumed that the king is a Christian (I. ii. 241, 2 Chorus 6; Chel., p. 82; Eras., *Prefatory Letter,* p. 177, etc.) and one who supports the Christian Church (I. i. 23, 73; Chel., p. 82; Eras., *passim*). He should be learned (I. i. 32, 38-47; Chel., p. 57, c. VI; Eras., *Prefatory Letter*) and well versed in theology (I. i. 38-40; Eras., p. 153). Justice should be established in his kingdom (II. ii; 2 *Henry IV,* v. ii. 43-145; Chel., p. 42, c. X; Eras., pp. 221-37) and he himself should show clemency (II. ii. 39-60; III. iii. 54; III. vi. 111-18; Chel., pp. 128-37; Eras., p. 209) not take personal revenge (II. ii. 174; Chel., p. 137; Eras., pp. 231-3) and exercise self-control (I. i. 241-3; Chel., p. 41; Eras., pp. 156-7). He should allow himself to be counselled by wise men (I. ii; II. iv. 33; Chel., c. VI; Eras., p. 156), and should be familiar with humble people (IV. i. 85-235; Chel., pp. 129, 131; Eras., p. 245) though as Erasmus points out he should not allow himself to be corrupted by them (p. 150). The king seeks the defence and preservation of his state (I. ii. 136-54; II. ii. 175-7; Chel., p. 148; Eras., pp. 160, 161, etc.), his mind is burdened with affairs of state (IV. i. 236-90; Eras., p. 160) which keep him awake at night (IV. ii. 264, 273-4, 289; Eras., pp. 162, 184, 244). The kingdom of a good king is like the human body whose parts work harmoniously and in common defence (I. i. 178-83; Chel., p. 166; Eras., pp. 175-6) and again like the orderly bee society (I. i. 183-204; Chel., pp. 18-21; Eras., pp. 147, 165) with its obedient subjects (I. i. 186-7; Chel., p. 21; cf. Eras., p. 236). He should cause idlers, parasites and flatterers to be banished or executed (the fate of Bardolph, Nym, Doll, etc.; Chel., *Prologue*; Eras., p. 194, etc.). The ceremony and insignia of a king are valueless unless the king has the right spirit (IV. i. 244-74;

---

[1] For convenience the translation of the *Institutio,* by L. K. Born, *The Education of a Christian Prince,* 1936, has been used.

Eras., pp. 150-2); some titles are mere flattery (IV. i. 269; Eras., p. 197); at all costs flattery is to be avoided (IV. i. 256-73; Chel., *Prologue*; Eras., pp. 193-204). Although it is customary to compare kings with great men of the past, the kings must remember that as Christians they are far better than such men as Alexander (IV. vii. 13-53; Eras., pp. 153, 203; cf. Chel., denunciation of Alexander for murdering Cleitus, p. 129). The king should consider his responsibility in war for causing the deaths of so many innocent people (IV. i. 135-49; Eras., pp. 253-4). The evils of war are described (II. iv. 105-9; III. iii. 10-41; V. ii. 34-62; Chel., pp. 169-71; Eras., pp. 253-4). It is a good thing for a king to enter into the honourable estate of matrimony (V. ii; Chel., p. 179).[2] Erasmus regards marriage for the sake of an alliance as liable to create further strife (pp. 241-3).

There are, too, some small points of resemblance. Chelidonius gives a full account of the society of bees (pp. 18-21) taken mainly from Pliny, *Nat. Hist.*, XI, and St. Ambrose, *Hexaemeron*, and his opening phrasing is similar to Shakespeare's, "they have their King and seeme to keepe a certaine forme of a kingdome," and he too stresses obedience as a civic virtue. The episode of the man who railed against Henry has a close parallel. Chelidonius, p. 137, refers to a story of Pyrrhus, king of Epirus, who pardoned some soldiers who spoke "uncomly and indecēt wordes of him" because they were drunk with wine.[3]

The Conversion of Prince Henry

It is just this portrait of Henry, the ideal king, that most commentators have found difficult to reconcile with Prince Hal, and to describe Henry as Hal "grown wise" is to avoid the issue. If *Henry V* is the end that crowns *1* and *2 Henry IV*, then King Henry V must come to terms with Prince Hal. The heart of the matter is the nature of the change that came over Henry at his coronation, and this must be examined in detail.

Shakespeare gives only one observer's account of what happened, that by the Archbishop of Canterbury I. i. 25-34:

> The breath no sooner left his father's body,
> But that his wildness, mortified in him,
> Seem'd to die too; yea, at that very moment,
> Consideration like an angel came,
> And whipp'd the offending Adam out of him,

---

[2] This part of the *Institution* was added by Bouvaisteau.
[3] Shakespeare, however, may have remembered the incident in Plutarch.

> Leaving his body as a paradise,
> T'envelop and contain celestial spirits,
> Never was such a sudden scholar made;
> Never came reformation in a flood,
> With such a heady currance, scouring faults.

This deftly intricate passage is based mainly on the Baptismal Service from the *Book of Common Prayer*. Compare,

> he being dead unto sin . . . and being buried with Christ in his death, maye crucifye the olde man, and utterlye abolyshe the whole bodye of sinne,

and,

> graunt that the olde Adam in this child may be so buryed, that the new man may be raised up in him,

and,

> that all carnall affections maye dye in him, and that all thynges belonginge to the Spirite may lyve and growe in him.[4]

Again the baptismal "washing away of sins" is almost certainly responsible for the flood imagery in ll. 32-4. Not only is Baptism the "only true repentance" in Jeremy Taylor's phrase, but it is also a means of "spiritual regeneration."

This, however, is not all. Lines 28-30, besides containing an obvious allusion to the casting forth of Adam and Eve from the Garden of Eden (*Gen*. iii. 23-4) have a deeper significance. The word "consideration" is usually glossed as "reflection" or "contemplation," but this is surely an unsatisfactory gloss here. Its usage in this period points to another connotation. In the *Authorized Version* the verb "consider" is frequently used where it is almost equivalent to an exhortation to repent from evil doing or at least in association with evil doing (*Deut*. xxxii. 29; *Ps*. l. 22; *Hag*. i. 5; *Isa*. i. 3; *Jer*. xxiii. 20; xxx. 24, etc.). In Donne's sermons "consideration" appears again with similar associations (*Sermons* XLV, LIV. §2, LXIII, etc.), as it does in Hooker (*Works*, 1850, II. 242). Jeremy Taylor, *Holy Living and Holy Dying* uses "consideration" in numerous section headings with the meaning of spiritual contemplation, and again in the general context of turning away from sin to the good life or the good

---

[4] *Boke of Common Prayer*, London, 1560.

death. It is evident that the word was associated with intense spiritual contemplation, and self-examination, and not with merely thought or reflection.

Centuries earlier Bernard of Clairvaux, called upon to write an exhortation that would encourage corrupt members of the Church to repent and reform their lives, wrote *De Consideratione*. "Consideration" for St. Bernard is one of the "creatures of Heaven" [5] dominated on earth by the senses. He notes that St. Paul's ecstasies (2 *Cor.* xii. 4) were departures from the senses and therefore forms of consideration or divine contemplation in which men were "caught up to Paradise." Consideration, when the help of heavenly beings is given—and such angelic help is given to those who are the "heirs of salvation" (*Heb.* i. 14)—becomes perfection in the contemplation of God. There is no evidence that Shakespeare knew Bernard's work, although it was regarded as one of his most important writings and was very highly esteemed in the Middle Ages. But the linking of significant words "consideration," "angel," "paradise," "celestial spirits," indicates that Shakespeare was undoubtedly thinking of repentance and conversion in the religious sense.

In a later comment on the Prince's reformation, Canterbury says,

> for miracles are ceas'd;
> And therefore we must needs admit the means
> How things are perfected.

Had it been doctrinally admissible Canterbury would have acknowledged a miracle; as it is, he has to admit that to the Prince by the revelation of divine grace is "made known the supernatural way of salvation and law for them to live in that shall be saved" (Hooker, *Eccles. Polity,* I. xi. 5).

Was there any suggestion of a religious conversion in the historical sources? Hall and Holinshed both state briefly that the Prince "put on the new man," a phrase that had become proverbial even in the sixteenth century and may therefore have lost its original scriptural significance. With two exceptions the earlier chroniclers are not very informative on this point; the exceptions are Elmham's *Liber Metricus* (p. 100), which gives a mere hint in the line "rex hominem veterem sic renovare" and the *Vita et Gesta Henrici Quinti,* written some thirty years after Henry's death. In this latter work, Henry, upon his father's death, spent the day in profound grief and repentance, he shed bitter tears and admitted his errors. At night he went secretly to a man of perfect life at West-

---

[5] Quotations taken from the translation of G. Lewis, 1908, pp. 130-7.

minster and received absolution. He departed completely changed "felici miraculo convertitur" (pp. 14-15). The writer of the *Vita et Gesta* has no doubt that there was a miraculous conversion.

It is not certain that Shakespeare was acquainted with the *Vita et Gesta*, but it is highly probable, at least as probable as that he knew the *Gesta*.

It may be objected that this does not solve the problem, but only introduces almost literally a *deus ex machina*. Yet if we had read *1* and *2 Henry IV* with imagination, this turn of events would not appear arbitrary and inconsistent. Let us reconsider some of Hal's speeches and actions in these two plays. In *1 Henry IV*, I. ii. 217-39, Hal's declaration that he would throw off his unyoked idle humour when the time was ripe and thereby gain wide approbation has earned him accusations of cold-hearted, selfish scheming. Admittedly the speech is a clumsy dramatic device which Shakespeare also used in *Richard III* to let Gloucester announce that he was "determined to prove a villain." But it is not cold-blooded scheming, it is a piece of self-extenuation, a failure to reform which Hal justifies as unconvincingly as Hamlet does his failure to run Claudius through while he was at prayer. It is no more and no less than St. Augustine's youthful prayer of repentance, "O God, send me purity and continence—but not yet." Henry's interview with his father brings about a partial change of his attitude, but he does not see beyond physical and material ends; his atonement is to match himself in battle with Hotspur, in which he succeeds brilliantly. These taken with Vernon's praise of him, *1 Henry IV*, v. ii. 51-68, suggest perhaps not altogether fancifully, that Henry had reached physical perfection, the first of Aristotle's three ways of perfection.

In *2 Henry IV*, II. ii. 51-61, we are given a clear warning not to think that Henry is a hypocrite, and in IV. iv. 67-78 Warwick's defence of the Prince's essential integrity. At the same time the Prince and Falstaff are moving farther apart, Hal has nothing to do with Falstaff's night of venery, nor with his capture of Coleville. The soliloquy on the cares of kingship shows the Prince beginning to realize his responsibilities; his profound grief (mentioned twice it should be noted), his reconciliation with his father, his committal of the powers of the law into the hands of the Lord Chief Justice, suggest again that he is attaining the second Aristotelian perfection, intellectual perfection, or as Hooker phrased it, "perfection civil and moral" (*Eccles. Polity*, I. xi. 4).

Finally, Canterbury's account in *Henry V* shows Henry's perfection, physical, intellectual and spiritual completed; he is now the "mirror of Christendom."

It could not be otherwise. Medieval and Tudor historians saw in the events they described the unfolding of God's plan, history for them was still a handmaid to theology, queen of sciences. Henry V, the epic hero and the agent of God's plan, must therefore be divinely inspired and dedicated; he is every bit as dedicated as is "pius Aeneas" to follow the divine plan of a transcendent God.

Within this all-embracing Christian Providence there was an acceptance of classical beliefs of the innate tendency of states to decay, and of the limitations and repetitions of human thoughts and emotions throughout the ages consequent on the sameness of the elements from which human bodies were formed. It was hoped that men would return to the brilliance of pagan achievement in classical times, that highest peak of human endeavour, since the conception of progress had not yet come to birth. In the meantime classical writers were models for imitation and touchstones of taste, classical figures were exemplars of human actions and passions, and the language of Cicero and Virgil, still current, foreshortened the centuries between. The modern was naturally compared with the ancient, Henry with Alexander. Calvary apart there could be no greater praise.

Only a leader of supreme genius bountifully assisted by Fortune and by the unity of his people could arrest this civic entropy and raise a state to prosperity. We do less than justice to Henry if we do not realize that in Elizabethan eyes he was just such a leader whose exploits were greater than those of other English kings, in Ralegh's words "None of them went to worke like a Conquerour: saue onely King *Henrie* the fift."

Shakespeare's Henry V

This is the man, and this his background. Let us now look more closely at Shakespeare's presentation of him in the major incidents of the play.

The conversation of Canterbury and Ely in the opening scene establishes economically the religious conversion of Henry on the highest authority in the country, Henry's support of the Church as a true Christian monarch, and his desire for guidance from learned churchmen, a procedure warmly recommended to kings by Erasmus, Chelidonius and Hooker. Later Canterbury demolishes the French objections to Henry's claim to the throne of France, and by his authority encourages Henry to undertake a righteous war. The characters of the two prelates have been heavily assailed, but Dover Wilson is surely right in his vindication of their integrity. Hall's bitter attack on the churchmen who sought to divert Henry's attention from the Bill by advocating war with France was followed more moderately by Holinshed.[6] Shakespeare, however, alters the order of events. Canterbury on behalf of Convocation offers Henry a subsidy to help him in the war with France which is already under consideration. His speech on the Salic Law is made at Henry's request to discover the truth behind the French objections to claims already presented, and not as in Hall and Holinshed thrust forward to divert his attention from the Lollard Bill by initiating a war with France. In 1585 in very similar circumstances the Earl of Leicester asked Archbishop Whitgift whether he should advise Queen Elizabeth to fight on the side of the Low Countries against Spain. There was talk, too, of seizing Church revenues to pay for the war, but nevertheless the Church encouraged the war and offered a substantial subsidy.[7] Moreover, to portray Henry as the dupe of two scheming prelates, or as a crafty politician skilfully concealing his aims with the aid of an unscrupulous archbishop, is not consistent with claiming at the same time that he is the ideal king; indeed it is destructive of the moral epic purpose of the play.

Yet Henry has been so calumniated. His invasion of France has been stigmatized as pure aggression—though the word is somewhat worn—and Henry himself charged with hypocrisy. Now Henry does not, as Bradley alleges, adjure "the Archbishop to satisfy him as to his right to the French throne," he urges that the Archbishop should

> justly and religiously unfold
> Why the law Salic that they have in France
> Or should, or should not, bar us in our claim

and the remaining thirty-two lines of his speech are a most solemn warning to the Archbishop not to

> wrest, or bow your reading,
> Or nicely charge your understanding soul
> With opening titles miscreate, whose right
> Suits not in native colours with the truth.

This does not sound like hypocrisy or cynicism. The Archbishop dis-

---

[6] Christopher Watson, *The Victorious actes of Henry the fift,* "coarcted out of Hall" goes further than Hall. He refers to the "panchplying porkheads" who to divert Henry's attention from the bill seek to "obnebulate his sences with some glistering vaile" (p. 100).

[7] Strype, *Life and Acts of Archbishop Whitgift,* I. 434. See L. B. Campbell, *Shakespeare's Histories,* p. 268.

charges his duty faithfully; as it stands his reasoning is impeccable apart from any warrant given by the precedent of Edward III's claims. Henry is not initiating aggression; in fact Shakespeare omits from Exeter's speech in Hall the one argument that has a predatory savour, namely, that the fertility of France makes it a desirable addition to the English crown. And if Shakespeare did consider Henry's claims justified, he was thinking in agreement with Gentili, the greatest jurist of the sixteenth century, who quite uninvited expressed his opinion that the claim of the English kings to the French throne was legal and valid:

> . . . as the kings of England wished to retain their rights in the kingdom of France . . . calling themselves their kings . . . and thus they preserve a kind of civil possession. . . . And that title is not an empty one . . . (*De Iure Belli,* p. 110).

Henry accepts the advice of his counsellors, but he it is who displays his foresight by asking the right questions. Shakespeare again adapts his sources to make Henry the first to raise the possibility of a Scottish invasion—not merely the incursion of marauding bands—during his absence in France, and then to assure himself of the essential unity of the country and its capacity to deal with such a threat.

In the presentation of the tennis balls by the French ambassadors Shakespeare has made a significant change from both Hall and Holinshed. Holinshed places the incident before Archbishop Chichele's speech in the Parliament of 1414, before there has been any suggestion of invading France; Hall places it after the speeches of Chichele, Westmoreland and Exeter, adding that, though he cannot be certain, this "vnwise presente" among other things may have moved Henry to be "determined fully to make warre in Fraunce." In the play it is placed *after* Henry has determined to make war in France, it makes no difference to the issue. Shakespeare uses it to show Henry's Christian self-control. To the French ambassadors, uneasy lest their message may cost them their lives, he declares:

> We are no tyrant, but a Christian king;
> Unto whose grace our passion is as subject
> As is our wretches fetter'd in our prisons.

The message itself he receives with unruffled urbanity:

> We are glad the Dauphin is so pleasant with us;
> His present and your pains we thank you for . . .

and wittily turns the jest on the sender. Henry, the ideal king, is not to be incited to war by a personal insult; he reveals remarkable self-restraint, at the same time warning the Dauphin that his refusal to treat the English claims seriously will bring about bloodshed and sorrow.

While with some insensitiveness to irony we in this modern age may excuse Henry's invasion of France as arising from his limited medieval horizons, many are less inclined to pardon his rejection of Falstaff. Although Shakespeare's original intention was to portray Falstaff larding the fields of France, no doubt discreetly distant from Henry, he must accept responsibility for the play as it is. If he were prohibited from introducing Falstaff in person into *Henry V*, why was it necessary to mention Falstaff at all? In some slight way it might be regarded as fulfilling the promise in the epilogue of *2 Henry IV* that Falstaff might "die of a sweat," or as containing a topical reference to the Oldcastle affairs, or as the best conclusion that could be made to cover the results of official interference; any or all of these might be offered as explanation. Surely the truth lies deeper. The "finer end" that Falstaff made changes the tone of the play, it deepens the emotion; indeed, it probably deepened the tone of the new matter in Act IV. The play gains in epic strength and dignity from Falstaff's death, even as the *Aeneid* gains from Dido's death, not only because both accounts are written from the heart with a beauty and power that have moved men's hearts in after time, but because Dido and Falstaff are sacrifices to a larger morality they both ignore. Some similarities too between Aeneas and Henry may be noted; both neglect their duties for pleasant dalliance; both are recalled to their duty by divine interposition; thenceforth both submit to the Divine Will —it is significant that in *Aeneid*, IV, 393, immediately after Dido's denunciation of him, Aeneas is "pius" for the first time in that book—both display a stoic self-control for which they have been charged with coldness and callowness.

Falstaff has given us medicines to make us love him; he has bewitched us with his company just as Dido bewitched the imagination of the Middle Ages. We have considered him at once too lightly and too seriously: too seriously in that we hold him in the balance against Henry and England, and too lightly in that as a corrupt flatterer he stands for the overthrow of the divinely ordained political order. Erasmus expresses the opinion of the age when he reserves his severest censures for those flatterers who corrupt a prince, the most precious possession a country has (p. 194), and whom he would punish with death. Falstaff is such a one. If Henry's conversion and acceptance of God's will mean anything at all, they must be viewed in the light of the period to see Henry's full stature, even as a reconsideration of Virgil's religion enlarges and dignifies the character of Aeneas. The medieval habit of mind did not disappear with the Renaissance and Copernicus, on the contrary it is no longer a paradox that the Renaissance was the most medieval thing the Middle Ages produced. For both Middle Ages and Renaissance religion was planned, logical and integrated with everyday life, not as it is for many of their descendants a sentimental impulse to an occasional charity. So while a place may have been found for Falstaff with his crew of disreputable followers with Henry's army, there could be no room for him in Henry's tent on the eve of Agincourt.

It has been suggested that Henry deals with the conspirators with cat-like cruelty. Now Shakespeare has deliberately added to his immediate sources the pardoning of the drunkard who reviled Henry and the merciless attitude of the conspirators towards this man. While the latter may owe something to Le Fèvre, there is nothing of the kind in Hall or Holinshed. The reason is clear enough. Henry is to be shown as the ideal prince magnanimous enough to pardon offences against his person like Pyrrhus, king of Epirus, and the conspirators are to blacken themselves by their contrasting lack of mercy. Even when to high treason Scroop adds the personal disloyalty of a beloved and trusted friend, a treachery that disgusted Henry's nobles, Henry, consistent with his mercy to the drunkard, seeks no personal revenge:

> Touching our person seek we no revenge;
> But we our kingdom's safety must so tender,
> Whose ruin you have sought, that to her laws
> We do deliver you.

Henry's threats to Harfleur sound horrible enough, but he was precisely and unswervingly following the rules of warfare as laid down by Vegetius, Aegidius Romanus, and others. Harfleur he regards as his rightful inheritance, and those who withhold it from him are "guilty in defence," because they wage an "impious war." [8] He allows the besieged time to discover whether a relieving force is on its way, then warns them to surrender before he begins his main assult which could not then be halted and which would have inevitable evil consequences. All this was in strict accord with military law:

> This also is the reason for the law of God which provides that cities which do not surrender before they are besieged shall not be spared (Gentili, *De Iure Belli,* p. 217).

[8] See note to III. iii. 15 [in Arden Edition].

Henry again exercises his royal clemency by requiring Exeter to "use mercy to them all."

It is in Act IV that we see the full picture of Henry as the heroic leader. The devotion and enthusiasm he inspires indeed begin earlier, before he set foot in France. His personality has united England as never before (I. i. 127), and already "the youth of England are on fire" eager to follow the "mirror of all Christian kings." Something of the expectation in the air of 1598, when Essex was preparing his forces for Ireland has infected the spirit of these lines. A contemporary describes such a gathering:

> They were young gentlemen, yeomen, and yeomen's sons and artificers of the most brave sort, such as did disdain to pilfer and steal, but went as voluntary to serve of a gaiety and joyalty of mind, all which kind of people are the force and flower of a kingdom.[9]

The heavy losses before Harfleur by battle and dysentery, the "rainy marching in the painful field," the frightening size of the French army which might well have disheartened Henry's men, only united them closer still. Henry shares their dangers and is accepted into their fellowship which his exhilaration and leadership had made so strong. He shares too in the grim jesting of men bound in spirit in the eye of danger, who hobnob sociably with the Almighty, of Lord Astley at Edgehill and of the English soldier at Fontenoy, who as the French troops levelled their firearms at the motionless English ranks, stepped forward and exclaimed, "For what we are about to receive may the Lord make us truly thankful." Henry's men are "taking no thought for raiment" for if God gives them victory they will have the coats off the Frenchmen's backs, and if not He will otherwise provide robes for them in Heaven.

Nobleman and common soldier alike are inspired by Henry's gay and gallant spirits. Among the English nobles there is a courteous loyalty to to each other quite unlike the sparrow squabbling of the French nobles, their preoccupation with vain boasting and their lack of foresight and order. Salisbury, the "winter lion" of 2 *Henry VI*, goes "joyfully" into battle, and Westmoreland unwishes five thousand of the men he had previously desired. Henry himself sums up the heart of the matter in the memorable words,

> We few, we happy few, we band of brothers,

words that have come to stand for so much that is English. Dover Wilson recalls Churchill's famous epitaph on those who "left the vivid air signed

---

[9] Quoted without reference, P. Alexander, *Shakespeare's Punctuation*, 1945, p. 1.

with their honour" in the summer of 1940, "Never in the field of human conflict was so much owed by so many to so few," as coming from the same national mint. But it is older than Shakespeare, it is pure Hall. Listen to his last words on Henry V:

> yet neither fyre, rust, nor frettying time shall amongest Englishmen ether appall his honoure or obliterate his glorye whiche in so fewe yeres and brief daies achived so high adventures and made so great a conquest.

The words are English but the mood is older and universal, it is the note of epic heroism that sounded at Thermopylae and in a pass by Rouncesvalles.

While Henry infuses courage into his men, he is not without unease of soul. The conversation with Bates, Court and Williams forces him to examine his conscience on his responsibility for those who are to die in the coming battle, and to complain how little his subjects understand the hard duties of a king in their interests. Militarily his position is desperate: his enemy has selected the time and place for battle, his men are heavily outnumbered, tired and weakened by disease and lack of food. His faith in the righteousness of his cause is strained to the uttermost, and in prayer he pleads that his father's sin of usurpation may not be remembered against him. His courage is magnificent, and his extraordinary self-control has not always been acknowledged. He does not unpack his heart and curse like a drab, nor flutter Volscian dovecots, nor unseam his enemies from the nave to the chaps, he is no tragic warrior hero, he is the epic leader strong and serene, the architect of victory.

For all his self-control he is moved to rage by the treacherous attack on the boys and lackeys in his tents, and, fearing for the safety of his army gives the harsh order to kill the prisoners. Dover Wilson's comment is valuable:

> The attack is historical; and Fluellen's exclamation, ' 'Tis expressly against the law of arms, 'tis as arrant a piece of knavery, mark you now, as can be offert!' is in accordance with much contemporary comment on the battle, which shows that the treacherous assault left a deep stain upon the chivalry of France. Thus any lingering doubt about Henry's action is blotted from the minds of even the most squeamish in the audience. . . .

Gower's remark, "the king most worthily hath caused every soldier to cut his prisoner's throat. O! 'tis a gallant king," shows wholehearted approval of Henry's promptness in decision and his resolute determination. The rage of the epic hero leading to the slaughter of the enemy within his power is not without Virgilian precedent (see *Aeneid*, X and XII).

Exeter's account of the deaths of York and Suffolk also touches Henry to tears. The purpose of the description, for which there is no warrant in any of the sources of the play, seems to have been overlooked. It is not, as has been supposed, an imitation of the moving and presumably successful description of the heroic deaths of Talbot and his son in *1 Henry VI*, IV. vi. and vii. York and Suffolk die in the right epic way, their love "passing the love of women" is fulfilled in death. The surviving heroes, in epic style, mourn their death at once so fitting, so sadly beautiful, so "pretty and sweet," a phrase recalling at once that other pair of heroes who "were lovely and pleasant in their lives, and in their death they were not divided."

The Henry of Act v is to many a disappointment, indeed the whole act, it is suggested, is an anticlimax. Dover Wilson defends it rather unconvincingly as a good mixture, and, following Hudson, praises Henry's overflowing spirits and frankness in the wooing scene as a convincing picture of the humorous-heroic man in love. This is so, but the truth lies deeper. The Christian prince to complete his virtues must be married. Bouvaisteau, following Aegidius Romanus, is most emphatic on this point. Erasmus agrees, though he discounts the value of alliances secured by marriage; in this he differs from other theorists. The brisk and joyous wooing promises a happy marriage, though both Henry and Katharine have themselves well under control. In fact, Henry's remark that the eloquence of Kate's lips moves him more than the eloquence of the French Council may be a glance at what some chroniclers openly stated, that Katharine's beauty was used to try to make Henry lessen his demands. Henry's earlier proverbial reference to himself as the king of good fellows may show that he fully appreciates this point that Katharine proverbially is the queen of beggars.

This marriage in particular seals the union of two Christian countries with momentous possibilities for Christendom then divided by schism. Henry's letter to Charles as related by Hall puts the matter clearly:

> Sometymes the noble ralmes of Englande & of Fraunce were united, whiche nowe be separated and deuided, and as then they were accustomed to be exalted through the vniuersall worlde by their glorious victories, and it was to theim a notable vertue to decore and beautifye the house of God . . . and to set a concorde in Christes religion (xliiiʳ).

The Treaty of Troyes saw Henry as the most powerful monarch in Europe, he had built unity by force of arms, by his inspiring military genius, and by the grace of God. He was now the complete Christian monarch, "the mirror of christendom." It is this completion that necessitated Act v, it was not implicit in Agincourt.

The character of Henry has not, of course, been "deduced" from the writings of Erasmus, Chelidonius and others, but it is significant that where Shakespeare adds to his historical sources, the intruding passage or episode has an apt parallel with passages from these writers. Even some of his omissions, notably the absence of reference to the English archers to whom the victory was mainly due, can be construed as helping to enlarge the stature of Henry. It is also not without significance that the Henry of *Henry V* is a complete and balanced contrast in character and appearance with Richard II in the first play of the tetralogy.

If Henry has proved less interesting a man than Richard, it is because his problems are mainly external. The virtuous man has no obvious strife within the soul, his faith is simple and direct, he has no frailties to suffer in exposure. It is just this rectitude and uprightness, this stoicism, this unswerving obedience to the Divine Will that links both Aeneas and Henry, and has laid them both open to charges of priggishness and inhumanity. Both are complete in soul:

> *omnia praecepi atque animo mecum ante peregi.*

Of Henry as of Aeneas can it truly be said,

> *rex erat . . . quo iustior alter*
> *nec pietate fuit, nec bello maior et armis.*
>
> [*Aeneid*, I. 554-5]

What Is Shakespeare's *Henry VIII* About?

by *Frank Kermode*

Discontent is the chief characteristic of all criticism concerned with *Henry VIII*, and it is not too much to say that a perennial incapacity to fit it into the shifting pattern of Shakespeare's life-work or to see it as a unified drama presenting distinct critical problems of theme and manner is responsible for the established habit of regarding it primarily as the centre of a merely scholarly dispute as to who wrote it, or who wrote which parts of it. I do not intend to hesitate over this aged argument any longer than is necessary to my theme; but since nearly all the criticism with which I am familiar regards the problem of authorship as inhibiting open discussion of that theme, it is essential to glance at the issue.

The notion that a good ear detects in the play stylistic variation so large that it can be reasonably accounted for only in terms of dual authorship is, I imagine, even older than Richard Roderick, who is given the credit of having first recorded it. We are warned, indeed, that good ears sometimes show remarkable disagreement among themselves, and are frequently, even on mature heads, full of echoes of a conservative school-teacher's forgotten instruction; but I cannot think that this is a caution sufficient to make most readers abandon the view that the splendours of the collapsing Buckingham and Wolsey, so relaxed and elegiac, so formal and so unstartling, are not Shakespearean splendours. A quick reference to the most conventional scenes of the *Winter's Tale* reveals the absence of such syntactically liberal verse; there is no conventional languor in Prospero's farewell to magic. I, for one, am not persuaded that there isn't an authorship problem.

I am, however, well aware that what I have said lacks the validity so

"What Is Shakespeare's *Henry VIII* About?" by Frank Kermode. From the *Durham University Journal*, n.s. IX (1948), 48-55. Reprinted by permission of the author and the *Durham University Journal*.

properly required in observations of this sort; the foregoing paragraph has a doubtful value as a subjective impression, but none at all (in isolation) as a contribution to objective truth. The issue is whether *any* observation of the internal "evidence" can have any more general validity than mine. Dr. Johnson's impression that the Prologue and Epilogue were not Shakespeare's was of precisely the same order as mine—*non vultus, non color* is the sum of his evidence, and the basis of his conjecture that the lines were the work of Jonson. Obviously such an issue could not be allowed to remain frankly at the mercy of conjecture, though in the absence of clear external evidence there was no way of avoiding exactly this kind of critical intuition as the *primum mobile* of all systematic work on the play; unfortunately its limitations as the starting-point of scholarly investigation were not invariably recognized.

This accounts for the famous investigation of Spedding, almost a century ago. Perhaps it is the lack of general interest in the play itself which is responsible for the survival of Spedding's essay as a central work in the study of it. In this case the basic intuition on which all the conjecture was based was due to no less good an ear than Tennyson's; and this celebrated organ detected in parts of *Henry VIII* the accents of Fletcher. Spedding proceeded to demonstrate, by means of "scientific" verse-tests of the kind just coming into vogue, that certain parts were indisputably by Shakespeare, certain others by Fletcher, and some more doubtful ones by Beaumont. His proof was pretty generally accepted, and, I suppose inevitably, gave rise to other work which credited Massinger with a hand in the play. It is precisely against the claims of the Spedding school that Professor Alexander argues in his contribution to the subject, of which more later. It is worth noting that Spedding, in taking up Tennyson's hint, discovered on reading the play that it was so patchy, discontinuous, and unshaped, that he was compelled to assume that one author had completed another's work without really knowing what the primary intention had been. I believe that this assumption of Spedding's underlies the dearth of critical comment on the play itself; it is assumed to be of interest only in that it was a collaboration of such a kind that no unity of conception and design ought to be expected of it. Even Alexander, in disposing of Spedding's proof, does not seriously challenge its corollary.

On the very general grounds that laymen are nowadays rather better educated in the matter of statistics than they were even fifty years ago, most people would regard Spedding's figures with some suspicion. The figures with which he deals are by no means large enough to convince us that analysis of them can offer "general formulæ which may be applied to any particular case considered." [1] So that even if the methods by which Spedding attempted to lift his thesis beyond mere conjecture were considered to be adequately precise, it is no longer possible to agree that they produce universally valid results. The more particular argument which Professor Alexander attacks in detail is that of Hickson, who held that one definitive test was provided by the fact that Fletcher sometimes, but Shakespeare never, "pauses upon a superabundant syllable." The way to disprove this assertion is, of course, to produce examples of the phenomenon from indisputably Shakespearean work; and this is what Professor Alexander does, though it is perhaps worth noting that not all his examples are good ones. Too many of them are drawn from lines broken between two speakers; examples of this sort can be found early in the canon, are not evidence that Shakespeare was changing his habits, and are, I think, unfair. His sixth example—

> Would have him wed again.
>   If you would not so—

is surely perfectly regular; an elision only (you'd) is required. Compare this line, occurring among the triplets of Jonson's Prologue to *Epicene*—

> And though all relish not, sure there will be some
> That when they leave their seats . . .

where there is presumably no doubt about the elision. It seems possible then (for others of Alexander's examples could be disputed) that it was not easy to collect many even in the later plays. Of course the Professor establishes his case, which is that "the extra accented syllable is . . . not unknown in Shakespeare's work," and the general pseudo-scientific structure which Spedding and his followers erected on that primary intuition of Tennyson or some other critic, such as themselves, has tumbled down. Nevertheless the intuition has precisely the same (limited) validity as it had before the assault. No amount of internal evidence could prove it right, and no amount will prove it wrong. And so, if it is profitless to talk about *Henry VIII* as an intelligible thing in itself unless single authorship can be proved (as Spedding assumed, and as Alexander assumed in confuting him), one might as well follow the tradition and give up at this point. But if we remind ourselves that Spedding accepted

---

[1] A mathematician, quoted in Alexander's article, "Conjectural History, or Shakespeare's *Henry VIII*" in *Essays and Studies* XVI, 1930, pp. 85-120. The argument is one with which Bernard Shaw has made many familiar.

the view that the play was unsatisfactory and formless *a priori,* and argued that proved collaboration would account for this state of affairs, and that this was most improper of him, since joint authorship doesn't inevitably produce discontinuity, and certainly not to the bizarre degree that this theory postulates (one collaborator not knowing what the other one was up to) we may take enough comfort from this apparent illogicality to proceed on another but more reasonable assumption, that, as has been previously but inadequately asserted, the play is substantially what one man would have written, even if more than one hand contributed to it.[2]

As I have indicated, I sympathise with Spedding when he expresses himself thus of his sensations in reading a scene written in a manner quite different from the preceding one—

> I felt as if I had passed suddenly out of the language of nature into the language of the stage, or of some conventional mode of conversation. The structure of the verse was quite different and full of mannerism. The expression suddenly became diffuse and languid. The wit wanted mirth and character. And all this is equally true of the supper scene . . .

although I should not have used language so gratuitously pejorative. The manner is different; there is no need to go beyond that. It is with this that I have to disagree—

> . . . throughout the play the king's cause is not only felt by us, but represented to us, as a bad one. We *hear,* indeed, of conscientious scruples as to the legality of his first marriage; but we are not made, nor indeed asked, to believe that they are sincere, or to recognise in his new marriage either the hand of Providence or the consummation of any worthy object, or the victory of any of those more common frailties of humanity with which we can sympathise. The mere caprice of passion drives the king into the commission of what seems a great iniquity; our compassion for the victim of it is elaborately excited; no attempt is made to awaken any counter-sympathy for *him;* yet his passion has its way, and is crowned with all felicity, present and to come. The effect is much like that which would have been produced by *The Winter's Tale,* if Hermione had died in the fourth act in consequence of the jealous tyranny of Leontes, and the play had ended with the coronation of a new queen and the christening of a new heir, no period of remorse intervening. It is as if Nathan's rebuke to David had ended, not with the doom of death

---

[2] Even Miss Spurgeon, in her British Academy Lecture *Shakespeare's Iterative Imagery* allowed herself to be diverted into discussing the authorship problem. Few would share her conviction that her methods offer a valuable test of authorship.

to the child just born, but with a prophetic promise of the felicities of Solomon
. . . I know of no other play in Shakspere which is chargeable with a fault
like this, none in which the moral sympathy of the spectator is not carried
along with the main current of action to the end.

All the same, this is the kind of criticism which lingers over Falstaff, the
fat loveable rogue, and calls Isabella a prig. It is almost enough to answer
that the play was by both necessity and choice obliged to be reasonably
historical. Anne was the mother of Elizabeth, and none of Katharine's
woes could alter the fact. Wotton called the play (the play that caused the
fire) by an alternative title, *All is True*; and the Prologue makes it plain
that foolery must be absent from a stage displaying what is "only true."
The time for taking liberties with the chronicles was past; and anyway
this history was much too recent to be drastically rebuilt. But this suggests that the play is a pageant with no more form than chronology imposes, and I am sure it is nothing of the sort. It is a new kind of play, and
very unlike the other histories, but not so unlike that they cannot help
us to understand it. Long before drama replaced the morality *rex* with
the King of England, but all about him stood the incarnate agents of his
and his land's good and evil. The Tudor king was God's deputy, and so,
of course, were the kings of the History Plays. But in every case there was
something wrong with their title and their rule; they were punished, or
their children's children were punished. Henry VIII, on the other hand,
had nothing wrong with his title, nor with his rule (if Halle and the
absence of judgment upon him may be believed) and as God's deputy
was a minister of grace. It is not he who rises and falls or merely falls
for the instruction of the audience; it is the Queen and various great
men under his rule. The play is concerned with the old tragic theme
of the great man's fall, and the King has a special place in that theme;
he is the centre of the drama (and therefore it is pointless to talk of having to get to know new characters at the end of the play) but he is not
simply the old *rex* who was the owner of the vices and virtues doing
battle about him; he is a representation of an exalted view of kingship
fostered by the Tudors out of expedience perhaps, but accepted by James
and his subjects as a natural law. If we recall that James himself is often
(especially in Court Masques) practically equated with God, and that
this is not to be written off as disgusting flattery, we may find it easier to
believe that Henry VIII is represented in this play as exercising certain
God-like functions.

   The Arden editor got nearer than most to seeing what the play was
about.

In comparison with *When you see me you know me*[3] the play may be regarded as history, but it is rather a new "Mirror for Magistrates" in the form of a drama, interspersed or interrupted by pageants. Those that can pity may, if they think it well, let fall a tear over the successive fates of Buckingham, of Wolsey, of Katharine; and for the sightseers there are the processions.[4]

No doubt the processions were conceived to meet a demand for spectacle, but they also have a simple function in the drama, which is to illustrate the circumstance from which the great ones fell. This is self-evident, and needs no labouring; the detail of the stage-directions indicates further that all is true. It is in regarding the play as a collection of tragedies that Pooler came near to the heart of the matter. For this is a collection of falls (Miss Spurgeon conscientiously notes the iterative imagery of falling) and there are not three falls, but four, Katharine's, Buckingham's, Wolsey's, and Cranmer's.

The tragedy of Katharine is the one which has provoked most indignant comment in the critics. We are made to sympathise with her; she clearly doesn't deserve to fall; Henry himself confesses her virtue—

> That man i' the world who shall report he has
> A better wife, let him in nought be trusted,
> For speaking false in that: thou art, alone
> If thy rare qualities, sweet gentleness,
> Thy meekness saint-like, wife-like government,
> Obeying in commanding, and thy parts
> Sovereign and pious else, could speak thee out,
> The queen of earthly queens. She's noble born,
> And like her true nobility she has
> Carried herself towards me.
>
> [II. iv. 134-143]

It is impossible to deny an element of hypocrisy in the King's character in this part of the play, or that he was too easily managed by flatterers. But this ought not to obscure the equal fact that there was reason in his stated motives for seeking the annulment, and that one of these, which would weigh powerfully with the Shakespearean audience, was the continued failure of Katharine to produce an heir. This was the reason, in

---

[3] Rowley's amusing play of 1605, which may be glanced at in the Prologue. It is, as Schelling says, the below-stairs view of the King. Will Summers is really the most important character. It shows Henry as bluff, choleric but addicted to jests.

[4] See Prologue, II. 5-7.

so far as reason was needed, for the stage-fall of this virtuous queen. In fact, the purely historical reason—after all, she did fall—was enough for the dramatist's purpose.

The *Mirror for Magistrates,* itself the product of a long medieval tradition, had a numerous progeny.[5] The theme continued popular until well into the Seventeenth Century; and by the turn of the century, so Farnham assures us, it was beginning to show its vitality and adaptability once more by allowing a discreet sentimentality to creep into it, especially when it was concerned with the Falls of Women. The tendency is discoverable in Daniel's *Rosamond* of 1592. Women were more likely to be the passive agents of evil than men, and philosophical considerations of the working of Fate, the natural concomitants of the *De Casibus* theme, could in these cases be suspended. So they are in Drayton's *Matilda* (1594), and the most powerfully sentimental of all such poems are Murray's *Sophonisba* (1611) and Sampson's *Fortunes Fashion* (1613) which concerns itself with the fall of Lady Elizabeth Gray, the queen of Edward IV. Sampson (whose work I have not read—it is very difficult to find) apparently treats his theme of injured innocence with a wealth of pathos, and Farnham believes that all this is symptomatic of the departure of the heroic spirit from literary tragedy, and its replacement by explorations of broken hearts and suffering womanhood.

Katharine's fall is surely exactly of this fashionable kind. She is presented happy and virtuous, confident of the King's attention, free-spoken and above all very much alive. At the prelates' enquiry she behaves much as Hermione does in *The Winter's Tale*; she firmly retains the sympathy of the audience which she won by her just forthrightness in the first Act. But she falls; there is no malice in the King when he considers it, and he sends her his good will before she dies. Griffith makes it clear that she deserves no reproach, and her death is heralded by a dance of blessed spirits. The whole scene in which the famous song is sung, and the death-scene itself, are full of carefully organised appeals to pity; the mood is elegiac; they are scenes of great beauty, but for all that they remain what are now known as "tear-jerkers." So were the poems of Murray and Sampson, practically contemporaneous productions; and this fall is the more pathetic in that it is *true.* Long before the *Mirror* itself had shown that British history was a rich storehouse of *De Casibus* exempla, no fiction could match history in this respect, for history shows what has happened and what therefore can and will happen again. Virtuous women fall; they are not without sin, and may be, as Katharine was, party to an

---

[5] See Willard Farnham: *The Medieval Heritage of Elizabethan Tragedy.* Berkeley, 1936.

offence perhaps incurring God's displeasure; but there is little suggestion
in this kind of tragedy that the fall is deserved. Fashion has, in this
corner of the traditional theme, ousted the customary moralising and
speculation. Katharine's ultimate beatitude is not in doubt; but on earth
she fell from greatness, though a queen and a king's daughter, and a
heavy spectacle it is.

The fall of Buckingham is a relatively simple affair. The spite of
Wolsey is the cause of it, and the sufferer, though a good and learned
man, is splenetic and undisciplined. The ultimate pathos of all such
falls is heavily underlined in this play. Buckingham makes a noble end,
in the tradition of English noblemen.

> For further life in this world I ne'er hope,
> Nor will I sue, although the king have mercies
> More than I dare make faults.
>
> > [II. i. 69-71]

When Vaux invites him to a barge fitting his great person, he replies—

> Nay, Sir Nicholas,
> Let it alone; my state now will but mock me,
> When I came hither I was lord high constable,
> And Duke of Buckingham; now poor Edward Bohun.
>
> > [II. i. 100-103]

Farnham's remarkable book makes us aware that the medieval view
of Fortune and its connexion with doctrines of divine retribution were
complicated and inconsistent. Fortune is sometimes a sporadic betrayer
of her minions; sometimes she inevitably makes fall succeed rise. To
ride her wheel was to make the whole circle; to fall rapidly from the
topmost point into the mire. That was the more general view, but the
first, that great men sometimes avoided falls, and wicked men punishment in this world, was also quite frequently proposed. The orthodox
Elizabethan view, however, denied Fortune existence except as a figura-
tive expression for God's providence. This was the view of Raleigh and
Primaudaye[6]—tragedy was explicable in terms of a man's sins and justice
operated inexorably in the sublunary sphere, for, as Aquinas held, the
divine providence prevented anything from occurring by chance. The
idea that, since good men fall and bad men escape earthly retribution,

---

[6] These doctrines are elucidated in R. W. Battenhouse's *Marlowe's Tamburlaine*,
Nashville, 1941.

there is an element of chance, and that, in a disordered world-centre, the provisions of Fortune operate but fitfully, was rejected by the orthodox as Epicurean; it was, in fact, an aspect of that Pyrrhonism to which the Protestant temper was naturally opposed. The orthodox view, as is well known, lies behind the sin-and-scourge pattern of the earlier histories. An ancient belief, which, Battenhouse suggests, survived through Plutarch, complicated the issue a little by holding that since man is fundamentally responsible for his own acts his wisdom can prevent his fall. But such a belief would be offset by Calvin's (whose affinities with Raleigh and Primaudaye as above expressed are obvious)—that man is incompetent, through *the* Fall, to behave so. Sin is inevitable, judgment is inevitable. The orthodox position is strong; but the misfortunes of good men were an observable fact, and though even good men are sinful there is an obvious disparity between a Buckingham or a Clarence on the one hand and a Wolsey or a Tresilian on the other. The *Mirror* itself, though much concerned with the idea that a great one rose by his crimes and perished by God's hand, did not claim that the just man would be free from effects indistinguishable from those of tragic retribution ("some have for their virtue been envied and murdered" it says, and perpetuates in some ways the old idea that against the cruelty of Mutability only the Stoic philosophy has a defence, regarding rise and fall and death itself as irrelevant. "Wherein may be seen by example how grievous plagues are punished, and how frail and unstable worldly prosperity is found, even of those whom Fortune seemeth most highly to favour"—be they just or not, one might add). I am sure the fall of relatively just men (it may easily be conceded that no man may be absolutely just) formed a separate group of tragedies even when the idea this kind of tragedy best exemplifies—*de Contemptu Mundi*—was moribund. In some ways the fall of Buckingham is the male equivalent of Katharine's fall, but it is altogether more conventional, closely resembles the kind of fall experienced in the original *Mirror* by Clarence, and lacks the elaborate fashionable circumstances of the Queen's tragedy. The pathos is certainly there; against the splendour of masquing and procession Buckingham has become plain Bohun; but, of course, we are not mulcted of so much sympathy for him as for the Queen, and he falls as great men will as the heterodox wheel turns.

Wolsey certainly does not fall "like a blessed martyr," and there is no difficulty in accounting for his tragedy in a perfectly orthodox way. He had been the protagonist of *De Casibus* tragedy long before this play was written. The prose *Life* of Cavendish, a gentleman usher in Wolsey's household, deliberately shaped the Cardinal's incredible rise and rapid fall on the Boccaccian model. Endowed with nothing but brains and a capacity for learning, his master rose on Fortune's wheel to the positions of King's chaplain, Archbishop of York, and Cardinal, to Chancellor of the Exchequer and the most powerful man in the kingdom, lavishing a great fortune on luxurious furnishings and entertainments of all kinds; but all this incurred him the animosity of powerful men, and he was in an instant swept away. (The play with its device of the inopportune discovery by the King of Wolsey's private accounts is not here historical, for it borrows the tale from another fall, of a Bishop of Durham who made this error and was exposed by Wolsey.) Finally the fallen man dies, broken by sickness. Cavendish, whose work was still in manuscript in 1613, though the author of this play must have had access to it, emphasises the odd fact that Wolsey's body was discovered to be clad in a hair shirt; and he makes it clear that in his view the Cardinal deserved his fame as well as his fall. In the play there is an obvious attempt in the speech of the gentle Griffith to do justice to the extraordinary magnanimity which was an aspect of Wolsey's obsession with power and greatness, but the author's animus is equally clear: Wolsey is associated with Rome, as Cranmer is with the Church of England; he calls Anne a spleeny Lutheran, whereas the well-disposed think of her as a jewel of worth. From Cavendish (to some degree aided by Campion) the conventional view of Wolsey probably derived. He was a great man, and fell greatly. So he is presented in the ambitious *Life and Death of Thomas Wolsey Cardinal* of Thomas Storer (1599) in which Farnham sees a prototype of the Elizabethan tragic pattern. Storer presents the tragedy as a clear case of rising, flourishing, and fallen greatness. In the play Wolsey is described as an example of purely malignant ambition meeting retribution not only through the discovery of his evil designs but from the accumulated animosity of the other lords who taunt him with his faults in a scene drawn in detail from Holinshed. Incidentally, it is the discovery of his traffic with the Pope which brings about his fall, and the fall was almost undoubtedly associated with the fall of the Roman Church in England. But it is basically as simple as the simplest and most orthodox falls in the *Mirror*, for Wolsey's acts of conspiracy and treachery are directly responsible for his tragedy, in that when they were discovered they provoked the just condemnation of the King, and also in that they roused the outraged earls who so gleefully accuse him (iii. ii.). This, then, is the completely orthodox fall, in accordance with contemporary Christian moral philosophy, and in a sense al the others are variants of it.

The most curious of these is the arrested fall of Cranmer. This seems to me the only possible description of it. Associated with it is the merely adumbrated fall of Gardiner, which is the product of the operation of Mercy in its negative mirror-image, Justice. For Cranmer (whose piety

is heavily emphasised in the first three scenes of the last Act) is evidently
headed for the same kind of fall as Buckingham's; he displays exemplary
resignation even before the event, exhibiting the humility and the traditional noble attitude of a man about to suffer. We are familiar with the
use of the figure of Fortune's buckets from *Richard II*, and just as there
is an element of this traditional imagery in the contrasting fortunes of
Katharine and Anne, so there appears to be in the supposedly falling
Cranmer and the overweening Gardiner. But the King, observing everything down to the indignities which Cranmer is made to endure, makes
an impressive entry and, having by use of the ring-token made it clear
to the enemies of the just cleric that he proposes personal intervention,
redeems Cranmer from falling and indicates a displeasure with Gardiner
and a recognition of his injustice which foreshadow retribution on this
arrogant (and Romish) antagonist.

This royal act is an exercise of mercy; and there is a connexion between the part here played by the King and the role of Mercy in the
earlier Moralities—that is, those written before the *tragic* theme usurped
the form, and in which *homo* in his extremity is preserved from Hell by
precisely such an act. It does not seem to me relevant to speak of in-
consistency in the character of the King, nor indeed to posit some act of
depersonalisation as so many modern critics might; for there is nothing
out of character in the exercise of divine grace by a Tudor or Stuart
sovereign. Here Henry is God's deputy, and it is well known that this
office was in Tudor political philosophy a property of all kings by divine
law. Cranmer and the Church of England redeemed, it is proper that he
should sponsor and prophesy over Elizabeth, the first personally effective
Protestant monarch, and the fact that she could not have existed but for
the tragedy of a good woman must not be allowed to detract from the
pleasure the auditors are expected to feel at the end of the play, which
is of course related to the happy dynastic progress of English history
since that birth, a progress which might have been very different if
Henry had not put away Katharine.

So the Arden editor is not far out when he suggests that this play is an
anthology of falls, like the *Mirror*. It is, however, as I see it, necessary to
count four of them. The last, Cranmer's, is different from the others. It
shows that a man having risen may avoid a fall because Mercy (and perhaps Wisdom as in the Plutarchian theory) intervene. It is not that retribution ceases to function; Cranmer was undeserving the treatment of
Wolsey. His fall would have been the kind which yields with any conviction only to the Pyrrhonist reading which was, though extant, heterodox. These four falls, all different, might well be regarded as an attempt

to present in the closest possible interrelation as many entertaining variants on the popular theme as the dramatic convention permitted.

Nevertheless, one should beware of regarding the play as episodic. It is called *Henry VIII* and it is about Henry VIII. Notoriously, kings were men as well as divine agents. Here is a king susceptible to flattery, to adulterous passions, choleric and extravagant. His rejection of Katharine is influenced by some of those human flaws; but it is not quite unconnected with a proper kingly concern over the health of the state. The result is the tragedy of a good woman, a type well understood, and for which the dramatist had exemplars. Human justice lacks the certainty of its divine counterpart; so, in spite of a fair trial, Buckingham, not without sin, falls. The man who caused this tragedy falls as a result of his treachery in the treatment of the affair of the Queen; he knows very well what the moral of his tragedy is, and urges it on Cromwell at some length. "Fling away ambition," he says, already seeing himself as an example or a Mirror. He was never happy until the fall occurred, for God has so disposed it that the evildoer has that in his own breast which destroys his peace. Here punishment is visited on the offender through the King; he is the agent of the divine retribution. As Wolsey falls in sin, Cranmer rises in virtue, and they clearly represent Popery and the English Church as much as they do great men vicious and virtuous. In his turn, Cranmer falls, and we have a pattern whereby to understand the nature of his tragedy; but there is no need for it; Mercy intervenes, and virtue is saved from such a tragedy by the King himself. The guilt or virtue of the King in respect of these happenings should be judged primarily by their fruits. These are the birth of a great queen and the establishment of the reformed church. It is unthinkable that these should be dismissed as the workings of chance; such a position would be both heterodox and treasonable. The play may be regarded as a late morality, showing the state from which great ones may fall; the manner of their falling, be they Good Queen, Ambitious Prelate, Virtuous Prelate, or merely Great Man; and the part played in their falls for good or ill by a King who, though human, is *ex officio* the deputy of God, and the agent of divine punishment and mercy.

Chronology of Important Dates

Note: The dates of plays refer to first performances and are based on G. E. Bentley, *Shakespeare: A Biographical Handbook* (New Haven: Yale University Press, 1961). Since there is no contemporary record of these performances, the dates should be taken as informed guesses.

1564	Shakespeare born at Stratford-upon-Avon; baptized April 26.
1582	Married to Anne Hathaway.
1583	Susanna born.
1584	The twins, Hamnet and Judith born.
1590-92	The three parts of *HENRY VI* performed in London.
1592	First printed reference to Shakespeare in London: Greene's satirical comment on *III HENRY VI*.
1592-93	*RICHARD III, The Comedy of Errors.*
1593-94	*Titus Andronicus, The Taming of the Shrew.*
1594-95	*Two Gentlemen of Verona, Love's Labor's Lost, Romeo and Juliet.*
1595-96	*RICHARD II, A Midsummer Night's Dream.*
1596-97	*KING JOHN, The Merchant of Venice.*
1597-98	The two parts of *HENRY IV.*
1598-99	*Much Ado about Nothing, HENRY V.*
1599	Building of the Globe Theater.
1599-1600	*Julius Caesar, As You Like It, Twelfth Night.*
1600-01	*Hamlet, The Merry Wives of Windsor.*
1601	Shakespeare's company hired by followers of Essex to play *RICHARD II* as propaganda for rebellion.
1601-02	*Troilus and Cressida.*
1602-03	*All's Well that Ends Well.*
1604-05	*Measure for Measure, Othello.*
1605-06	*King Lear, Macbeth.*
1606-07	*Antony and Cleopatra.*
1607-08	*Coriolanus, Timon of Athens.*
1608-09	*Pericles.*
1609-10	*Cymbeline.*
1610-11	*The Winter's Tale.*

1611-12	*The Tempest.*
1612-13	*HENRY VIII, The Two Noble Kinsmen.*
1613	Globe Theater burned down during a performance of *HENRY VIII* June 29
1616	Shakespeare died April 23.
1623	First Folio edition of Shakespeare's plays.

Notes on the Editor and Authors

EUGENE M. WAITH, the editor of this volume, is Professor of English at Yale University. He has edited *Macbeth* for "The Yale Shakespeare" and *Bartholomew Fair* for "The Yale Ben Jonson," and is the author of *The Pattern of Tragicomedy in Beaumont and Fletcher* and *The Herculean Hero.*

LILY B. CAMPBELL, now retired from the University of California at Los Angeles, where she was Professor of English, is the author of many articles on Elizabethan literature and of *Scenes and Machines on the English Stage* and *Shakespeare's Tragic Heroes, Slaves of Passion.*

The late E. M. W. TILLYARD, Master of Jesus College, Cambridge, where he was also a University Lecturer in English, was the author of many books on Shakespeare and Milton and of *Poetry Direct and Oblique, The English Epic and its Background,* and *The English Renaissance, Fact or Fiction?*

M. M. REESE is the author of *The Tudors and Stuarts* and *Shakespeare: his World and his Work.*

J. P. BROCKBANK is Professor of English at the University of York. He has edited Pope's poetry and written critical studies of Shakespeare and Marlowe.

A. P. ROSSITER, author of *English Drama from Early Tudor Times to the Elizabethans,* was best known as a lecturer on the B. B. C., in Cambridge, where he was a University Lecturer in English, and in Stratford-upon-Avon, where he was a frequent visiting lecturer.

JAMES L. CALDERWOOD is Assistant Professor of English at the University of California at Los Angeles. He has published articles on Shakespeare, Chaucer, Webster, and Swift.

DEREK TRAVERSI, who has recently held overseas posts in the British Institute and British Council, is the author of *An Approach to Shakespeare* and, most recently, of *Shakespeare: The Roman Plays.*

R. J. DORIUS, recently guest Professor of English at the University of Hamburg, is Associate Professor of English at San Francisco State College. He is the editor of *Henry V* in "The Yale Shakespeare."

J. DOVER WILSON, now retired from the University of Edinburgh, where he was Regius Professor of Rhetoric and English Literature, has been a prolific editor and author. Several of his works are mentioned in the introduction and the bibliography; among the others are *What Happens in Hamlet* and, more recently, *Shakespeare's Happy Comedies* and *Shakespeare's Sonnets.*

J. H. WALTER is the editor of the "Players' Shakespeare" and of two seventeenth century plays, *Charlemagne* and *The Launching of the Mary* for "The Malone Society Reprints."

FRANK KERMODE, John Edward Taylor Professor of English at the University of Manchester, has edited *The Tempest* for "The Arden Shakespeare." Among his critical studies are *John Donne, English Pastoral Poetry,* and *The Romantic Image.*

Selected Bibliography

Some of the most important basic studies are described in the Introduction, and those by Lily B. Campbell, M. M. Reese, E. M. W. Tillyard, and J. Dover Wilson are represented in this volume by substantial excerpts. Several articles that could not be included are also mentioned in the Introduction. There is a useful bibliography in Irving Ribner's *The English History Play in the Age of Shakespeare* (Princeton, New Jersey: Princeton University Press, 1957) and, as noted in the Introduction, Harold Jenkins has an extensive review of twentieth century scholarship in *Shakespeare Survey*, VI (1953), 1-15. Many sorts of information will be found in J. Dover Wilson's editions of the history plays for "The New Shakespeare" (Cambridge University Press) and in the revised volumes of "The Arden Shakespeare" (Methuen and Co. Ltd.).

The following brief selection from the vast literature on these plays is limited to essays on a few special problems and arranged accordingly:

J. Dover Wilson and T. C. Worsley, *Shakespeare's Histories at Stratford 1951*. New York: Theatre Arts Books, 1952. An essay by Dover Wilson on Elizabethan attitudes toward history and an illustrated discussion by the drama critic of the *New Statesman* of the second tetralogy in performance.

A. C. Bradley, "The Rejection of Falstaff," *Oxford Lectures on Poetry*, 2d. edition (London: Macmillan and Co. Limited, 1950), pp. 247-73. A famous essay by the author of *Shakespearean Tragedy*, arguing that the rejection reveals the unpleasant side of the Prince.

E. E. Stoll, "Falstaff," *Shakespeare Studies* (New York: G. E. Stechert & Co., 1942), pp. 402-90. An attempt to counter the interpretations of Morgann and Bradley by referring to the "braggart warrior" tradition.

J. I. M. Stewart, "The Birth and Death of Falstaff," *Character and Motive in Shakespeare* (London: Longmans, 1949), pp. 111-39. A review of earlier criticism and an interpretation in the light of the archetypal pattern of ritual slaying.

Arthur Sewell, "Character and Social Order," *Character and Society in Shakespeare* (Oxford: The Clarendon Press, 1951), pp. 35-52. A valuable study of the relationship between the concept of order and characterization in some of the comedies and histories.

G. K. Hunter, "*Henry IV* and the Elizabethan Two-Part Play," *Review of English Studies*, n.s. V (1954), 236-48. In the light of other two-part plays, *Henry IV* is seen to have the parallel structure of a diptych.

Harold Jenkins, *The Structural Problem in Shakespeare's Henry the Fourth*. London: Methuen and Co. Ltd., 1956. A lecture reviewing the controversy about the unity of the two parts and suggesting that Shakespeare changed his plan.

Paul Jorgenson, *Shakespeare's Military World*. Berkeley and Los Angeles: University of California Press, 1956. A study of Elizabethan military practice and contemporary attitudes toward war and peace in relation to Shakespeare's plays.

L. C. Knights, "Time's Subjects: The Sonnets and *King Henry IV, Part II*," *Some Shakespearean Themes* (London: Chatto & Windus, 1959), pp. 45-64. An analysis of tone and theme which relates the play both to the Sonnets and to the great tragedies.

Wolfgang Clemen, "Anticipation and Foreboding in Shakespeare's Early Histories," *Shakespeare Survey*, VI (1953), 25-35; "Tradition and Originality in Shakespeare's *Richard III*," *Shakespeare Quarterly*, V (1954), 247-57. Two acute discussions of style and structure in the first tetralogy.

————, "Popular Drama and History Plays," *English Tragedy Before Shakespeare* London: Methuen and Co. Ltd., 1961), pp. 192-210. A study of the form and style of some early non-Shakespearean history plays.

TWENTIETH CENTURY VIEWS

BRITISH AUTHORS